English G 21

A3

Freiarbeitsmaterialien
Kopiervorlagen

Cornelsen

English G 21

Freiarbeitsmaterialien
A3
Kopiervorlagen

Im Auftrag des Verlages herausgegeben von
Prof. Hellmut Schwarz, Mannheim

Erarbeitet von
Eva Ernst-Redeker, Krefeld
Nicole Schüttauf, Essen

In Zusammenarbeit mit der Englischredaktion
Dr. Christiane Kallenbach (Projektleitung);
Nathalie Schwering (verantwortliche Redakteurin)

Illustration
Henning Ziegler, Berlin

Titelbild
IFA-Bilderteam, Ottobrunn (Union Jack:
Jon Arnold Images)
Henning Ziegler, Berlin (Illustration)

Umschlaggestaltung und Layoutkonzept
Klein & Halm Grafikdesign, Berlin

Layout und technische Umsetzung
MatMil Translations & Desktop Publishing, Berlin

www.cornelsen.de
www.EnglishG.de

1. Auflage, 1. Druck 2009

© 2009 Cornelsen Verlag, Berlin

Das Werk und seine Teile sind urheberrechtlich geschützt. Jede Nutzung in anderen als den gesetzlich zugelassenen Fällen bedarf der vorherigen schriftlichen Einwilligung des Verlages.
Hinweis zu den §§ 46, 52 a UrhG: Weder das Werk noch seine Teile dürfen ohne eine solche Einwilligung eingescannt und in ein Netzwerk eingestellt oder sonst öffentlich zugänglich gemacht werden.
Dies gilt auch für Intranets von Schulen und sonstigen Bildungseinrichtungen.

Die Kopiervorlagen dürfen für den eigenen Unterrichtsgebrauch in der jeweils benötigten Anzahl vervielfältigt werden.

Druck: CS-Druck CornelsenStürtz, Berlin

ISBN 978-3-06-032267-1

Inhalt gedruckt auf säurefreiem Papier aus nachhaltiger Forstwirtschaft.

Vorwort

Autonomie im Unterricht

Die vorliegenden Materialien zur Freiarbeit bieten den Schülern vielfältiges Material zur spielerischen Überprüfung gelernter Inhalte an. Dies ist für die Schüler gerade im Hinblick auf die weithin geforderte Lernerautonomie von großer Bedeutung.

Freiarbeit bedeutet vor allem selbstbestimmtes Arbeiten. Die Schüler werden dabei schrittweise dazu befähigt, Verantwortung für das eigene Lernen zu übernehmen. Sie haben hier die Möglichkeit, das eigene Lerntempo zu bestimmen.

Alle Materialien können von den Schülern anhand des Lösungsschlüssels am Ende des Heftes selbst überprüft werden, so dass der Lehrkraft an dieser Stelle des Unterrichts mehr die Rolle des Lernberaters zukommt. Die Lehrkraft kann sich dadurch vor allem den schwächeren Schülern zuwenden und unterstützend tätig werden. Auch sollte die Lehrkraft darauf achten, dass sich die Schüler bei Partner- und Gruppenarbeit in der Zielsprache austauschen und die angegebenen Redewendungen benutzen.

Spielerischer Lernprozess

Die vorliegenden Freiarbeitsmaterialien bieten oft spielerische Ansätze und sollen die Schüler dazu motivieren, sich mit der Zielsprache zu beschäftigen. Die Sammlung enthält neben Spielen auch Partnerarbeitsmaterialien, um das gemeinsame Lernen zu fördern. Wenn die Klassensituation dies ergibt, können bei Partnerübungen z.B. ein schwächerer und ein stärkerer Schüler zusammenarbeiten, wobei der stärkere dem schwächeren Schüler Hilfestellung bietet und dadurch auch sein eigenes Wissen festigt.

Binnendifferenzierung

Gerade in Klassen mit einem breiten Leistungsspektrum bieten sich die Freiarbeitsmaterialien auch für den Einsatz bei der Binnendifferenzierung an. So werden schwächere Schüler individuell gefördert und stärkere Schüler gefordert.

Zielgruppe

Die Freiarbeitsmaterialien sind für die Gymnasialausgabe von English G 21, Band 3, konzipiert und unitweise aufgebaut. Die Materialien können sowohl einzeln als auch in Partnerarbeit bearbeitet werden. Langfristig wird so die soziale Kompetenz gefördert. Es ist von entscheidender Bedeutung, dass sich die Schüler gegenseitig helfen und korrigieren.

Benutzung der Materialien

In den Übersichtsseiten vor den Units wird der jeweilige Schwerpunkt der einzelnen Arbeitsblätter kenntlich gemacht. Dieser kann auf Grammatik, Redemitteln, oder Wortschatz liegen. Dadurch können die Materialien sowohl im normalen Unterricht zur Vertiefung eines Schwerpunkts oder zur Wiederholung eingesetzt werden, ebenso wie in ausgewiesenen Freiarbeitstunden.

Dort, wo etwas ausgeschnitten werden muss, wurde dies durch das Symbol der Schere kenntlich gemacht. Es bietet sich an, die Materialien zu folieren, um sie haltbar zu machen.

Inhalt

Unit-Überblick

Unit 1 – Überblick 8

Unit 2 – Überblick 20

Unit 3 – Überblick 31

Unit 4 – Überblick 38

Unit 5 – Überblick 50

Lösungen .... 60 – 67

Kopiervorlagen

	Nummer	Titel	Schwerpunkt
Introduction	0.1	Introduction: Music for you(th)	Wortschatzübung zum Thema *music*.
Unit 1	1.1	Town and transport	Wortschatzübung zu den Themen *town* und *transport*.
	1.2	Toby's homework	Grammatikübung zur Wiederholung der *irregular verb forms*, *simple past* und *present perfect*.
	1.3	Since when and for how long?	Grammatikübung zur Verwendung des *present perfect* mit *since* und *for*.
	1.4	London sights	Übungen zur Lesekompetenz und zur Festigung landeskundlichen Wissens über London.
	1.5	Planning a day in London	Vertiefung des landeskundlichen Wissens über London mit einer die Schreibkompetenz fördernden Aufgabe.
	1.6	A postcard from London	Hier wird das Überarbeiten eines selbst verfassten Textes in Bezug auf Aufbau und Verknüpfung der Sätze geübt.
Unit 2	2.1	Focus on words: Electronic media	Wortschatzübung zum Thema *electronic media*.
	2.2	Focus on grammar: My diary	Grammatikübung zum *present progressive with future meaning*.
	2.3	Focus on grammar: What will the future be like?	Grammatikübung zur Wiederholung des *will-future*.
	2.4	Focus on grammar: Spontaneous	Grammatikübung zur Verwendung des *will-future* bei spontanen

		decisions	Entscheidungen.
	2.5	Focus on grammar: What would you do?	Grammatikübung zur Verwendung des *conditional II* im *if-clause*-Gefüge.
	2.6	Proverbs and morals	Übung zur Verwendung des zweisprachigen Wörterbuchs anhand idiomatischer Sprichwörter.
Unit 3	3.1	Focus on words: Sport	Wortschatzübung zum Thema *sport*.
	3.2	Focus on grammar: Relative clauses	Grammatikübung zur Verwendung der *relative pronouns* und *relative clauses*.
	3.3	Focus on grammar: Contact clauses	Grammatikübung zur Verwendung der *contact clauses*.
	3.4	Focus on grammar and writing: The passive voice	Grammatikübung zur Bildung und Verwendung von Passivformen.
	3.5	Test your knowledge	Grammatikübung zur Verwendung des Passivs im *simple past*.
	3.6	Writing a report on your last class trip	Vertiefungen der Schreibkompetenz anhand eines Berichts über den letzten Klassenausflug.
Unit 4	4.1	A crossword on Canada	Wortschatzübung zum Thema *Canada*.
	4.2	Revision: The Passive	Grammatikübung zur Wiederholung des Passivs.
	4.3	Focus on grammar: Simple past and past perfect	Grammatikübung zur Verwendung des *simple past* und *past perfect*.
	4.4	Focus on grammar: Indirect speech	Grammatikübung zur Festigung des Gebrauchs der *indirect speech*.
	4.5	Mediation: A Telephone conversation	Übung zur Festigung der *mediation skills*.
	4.6	Writing a story	Mehrschrittige Schreibaufgabe zur Festigung der *steps of writing*.
Unit 5	5.1	Focus on words: Music, stars and instruments	Wortschatzübung zu den Themen *music, stars* und *instruments* mit anschließender Schreibaufgabe.
	5.2	Talking about oneself – my own biography	Schreibaufgabe: Verfassen eines autobiografischen Textes.
	5.3	Focus on grammar: Refelxive pronouns and verbs	Grammatikübung zur Verwendung der *modals* und ihrer Ersatzformen.
	5.4	Modal substitutes: Can, must and may	Grammatikübung zur Verwendung der *modal substitutes*.
	5.5	Focus on grammar: Conditional III	Grammatikübung zur Verwendung des *conditional III*.
	5.6	Writing about a star	Schreibaufgabe: Interview und Biografie.

0.1 KV Introduction: Music for you(th)

My favourite summer song this year is …

I listen to the radio when …

This is why I can't live without music: …

I like the lyrics of the song: because …

Finish!

Start

What is your favourite band or singer?

Which instrument do you (want to) play?

Introduction: Music for you(th) KV 0.1

I think classical music is …

I want to go to a concert of this band: …

My parents listen to …

My mp3 player is always with me when I …

If I want to be happy, I listen to …

- Play the game in groups of three or four.
- You will need some counters.
- When it´s your turn, move forward one field.
- Answer in a complete sentence, or you will have to stay where you are.
- Every answer takes you one field forward.
- The first one to reach the finish wins the game.

Enjoy the game!

This song is the worst song I know: …

Which instrument do you not like at all?

Which types of music do you know?

Unit 1 – Überblick

KV 1.1 Town and transport

In diesen Übungen wird der Wortschatz zum Thema Stadt und Verkehrsmittel vertieft und gefestigt. Dabei festigen die S ausgehend vom einzelnen Begriff über feststehende Ausdrücke bis hin zum Kontext des gesamten Satzes schrittweise ihr Wissen.

KV 1.2 Toby's homework

In dieser Übung werden die *irregular verb forms* auf Basis des A2-Schülerbuchs mit Einsetzübungen zu *simple past, present perfect* und deren Verneinungen wiederholt. Außerdem werden hier noch einmal die Signalwörter wiederholt.

KV 1.3 Since when and for how long?

In diesen Übungen geht es um die Verwendung des *present perfect* vor allem in Kombination mit *since* und *for*.

KV 1.4 London sights

In dieser KV wird die Lesekompetenz geschult und anhand von *true-false-questions* überprüft. Darüber hinaus wird das landeskundliche Wissen vertieft und in einer Schreibaufgabe gefestigt. Darin werden Vorlieben versprachlicht und Begründungen in der Fremdsprache formuliert.

KV 1.5 Planning a day in London

In dieser KV soll das landeskundliche Wissen vertieft werden. Der Schwerpunkt liegt auf den *writing skills*. Methodisch geht es bei hierbei um die sukzessive Ansammlung von Informationen und deren geordnete Wiedergabe in einem Fließtext.

KV 1.6 A postcard from London

In dieser KV wird das sinnvolle Verknüpfen von Ideen geübt, indem ein verbesserungswürdiger Text in Bezug auf seinen Aufbau und seine Verknüpfungen optimiert werden soll.

Town and transport KV 1.1

a) Look at the pictures and fill in the crossword.

Schau dir die Bilder an und fülle das Kreuzworträtsel aus!

Seite 1 von 2

1.1 KV Town and transport

b) Now match the words from the crossword with the right verbs.

Nun verknüpfe die Wörter aus dem Kreuzworträtsel mit passenden Verben.

(to) take	the bus, the train, …
(to) wait for	
(to) wait at	
(to) get on / off	
(to) go to	
(to) buy	
(to) pay for	
(to) be at	
(to) watch	

c) Fill in the gaps.

1 Many people _____ (gehen in die Kirche) on Sundays

2 Let's _____ (den Zug nehmen) to London, not the bus.

3 Many years ago there were still _____ (Straßenbahnen) in London. Now there are only buses and the tube.

4 Tony fell off his bike. After that he _____ (war im Krankenhaus) for a week.

5 There's a regular _____ (Fähre) service between Ostende and Dover.

6 Trains from Brighton go to Victoria _____ (Bahnhof) in London.

7 Let's _____ (ins Kino gehen) and watch a good film.

8 You can _____ (Fahrkarten kaufen) at the ticket machine.

9 Heathrow is a big _____ (Flughafen) near London.

10 Let's go to the airport and _____ (Flugzeuge anschauen).

11 Come on, Peter, we have to _____ (aus dem Bus aussteigen) at the next stop.

Toby's homework KV 1.2

a) Toby hasn´t finished his homework yet. He needs the verb forms to do it.
Can you complete the table with the missing forms?

*Toby hat seine Hausaufgaben nicht fertig. Er braucht die Verbformen, um sie zu erledigen.
Kannst du die fehlenden Verbformen in die Tabelle eintragen?*

to write	*wrote*	*written*	*schreiben*
		stood	
	sang		
to ring			
		ridden	
to find			
		eaten	
			kaufen
		given	
to pay			
	wrote		
			trinken
to teach			
		took	
	did		

b) Now Toby can do his homework much better. He needs to fill in the gaps
with the right verb forms. Can you help him?

*Nun kann Toby seine Hausaufgaben viel besser erledigen. Er braucht nur die richtige Verbform
in die Lücken einzutragen. Kannst du ihm dabei helfen?*

1

What have you already done today?

1 I have already _____ my sandwich.

2 We have already _____ an essay in English.

3 The pupils have already _____ in the music lesson.

2

What haven't you done yet?

1 I haven't _____ my homework yet.

2 We haven't _____ our tea yet.

3 My best friend hasn't _____ her horse yet.

1.2 KV Toby's homework

3

What did you do yesterday?

1 I _____ the books to the library.

2 We _____ the dogs their food.

3 My sister _____ her best friend on her mobile phone.

4

What didn't you do yesterday?

1 I really didn't _____ your chocolate!

2 Simon didn't _____ for lunch at school.

3 Our teacher didn't _____ us any homework.

c) Toby asks himself: "Which tense are the first two boxes in? Which tense are the last two boxes in?" Do you know the answers?

Toby fragt sich: „In welcher Zeit stehen die ersten beiden Boxen, in welcher die letzten beiden?" Kennst du die Antworten?

Box 1 and 2: _____

Box 3 and 4: _____

d) Toby is happy, he only needs to put the signal words into the boxes above. That's easy for you, isn't it?

Toby freut sich, nun muss er nur noch die Signalwörter in die Boxen hinter den Zeiten sortieren. Das fällt dir leicht, oder?

> ever • often • yesterday • always • last year
> already • in 1989 • never • last weekend
> not ... yet • a week ago • just • ...

Since when and for how long? KV 1.3

a) *Ask your partner about the gaps in your chart and fill in the answers.
Then answer your partner's questions.*

*Frage deinen Partner nach den dir fehlenden Informationen und notiere sie dir.
Dann beantworte die Fragen deines Partners.*

Partner A: Has Mary ever played an instrument?
Partner B: No, she hasn't.

Partner A:

	do judo	play an instrument	collect stamps	be a member of a local computer club
Mary	√			×
Chris			×	
Thomas	√	×		
Nick	√		×	√
You				
Your partner				

✂---

Partner B:

	do judo	play an instrument	collect stamps	be a member of a local computer club
Mary		×	√	
Chris	×	√		×
Thomas			×	√
Nick		×		
You				
Your partner				

1.3 KV Since when and for how long?

b) *Now swap your charts and check!*
   Nun tauscht die Tabellen aus und überprüft die Ergebnisse!

Remember:
- since + Zeitpunkt (e.g. last Monday, 2pm, …)
- for + Zeitspanne (e.g. five minutes, two years, …)

c) *Fill in **since** or **for**.*
   *Trage **since** oder **for** ein!*

1. Mary has done judo _____ 2006.
2. She has collected stamps _____ four months.
3. Chris has played an instrument _____ three years.
4. Thomas has done judo _____ January 2007.
5. He has been a member in a local chess club _____ one year.
6. Nick has done judo _____ last summer.
7. He has been a member of a local chess club _____ eight months.

d) *What have the people been doing for …/since …? Look at the picture and write sentences about the people in the picture. It's now 3pm. Say what the people have been doing and for how long. Use the present perfect progressive. You can choose between **since** and **for**.*

   *Schau dir das Bild an und schreibe über die Personen, die du siehst. Drücke aus, was die Personen tun und wie lange bereits. Benutze das present perfect progressive. Du kannst zwischen **since** und **for** wählen.*

Example: *Anna has been waiting for the bus since 2.50.*

London sights KV 1.4

a) *Read the following texts about sights in London for gist. Then think of a headline for each text.*

Madame Tussauds: _____

Madame Tussauds is a London museum which shows wax figures of famous people from the past and the present. Every year, more than two million tourists wait for hours to see the wax figures. There are more *Madame Tussauds* museums in Amsterdam, Berlin, Hollywood, Hong Kong, Las Vegas, New York, Shanghai and Washington DC.
But do you know who Madame Tussaud was? No? Well, Marie Tussaud was born in 1761. She made wax figures at a show in Paris for more than 20 years before she became the owner in 1794. She was famous for the masks she made of dead people's heads in the French Revolution. In 1802 she left France with her two sons and took the wax show to Britain. For the next 30 years the wax figures were shown all around the country. Then, in 1835, they were moved to London. Today, you can find her museum not far from the original place in Marylebone Road, London. There are wax figures of famous people in English history, like kings and queens, but also film stars like Nicole Kidman, cultural figures such as Einstein, musicians (for example Madonna) and sports stars like David Beckham.

Camden Market: _____

Camden Market is one of the most famous and biggest markets in London. You find it in Camden Town, a part of London, and about half a million people go there every week! You can get everything there: clothes, food, art, … But there are also many nice restaurants, theatres and bars. Take a walk along the canal and find the original *Camden Lock Market*, a craft market, which was established in 1974.
The markets and shops are open every day of the week and so it's always a good idea to go there. Just take the underground and get off at Camden Town station.

b) *Read the two texts again, this time for detail. Which statements below are true, which ones are false? Correct the false statements!*

1. Madame Tussaud was originally from France. ☐ True ☐ False
   _____

2. Madame Tussaud went to America in 1802. ☐ True ☐ False
   _____

3. There are wax museums in 10 other cities, too. ☐ True ☐ False
   _____

4. Today, there are wax figures of famous animals, too. ☐ True ☐ False
   _____

5. Camden Market is a famous London fish market. ☐ True ☐ False
   _____

6. You can't buy things there on Sundays. ☐ True ☐ False
   _____

7. In the evening, you can go to restaurants, too. ☐ True ☐ False
   _____

1.4 KV London sights

c) Now it's time to collect all the London sights you know.
Then put the sights in order from most interesting to least interesting.

Sammle nun Sehenswürdigkeiten Londons, die du kennst. Sortiere die Liste und setze die nach oben, die du am interessantesten findest. Ende mit denen, die dich am wenigsten interessieren.

Collection of London sights:

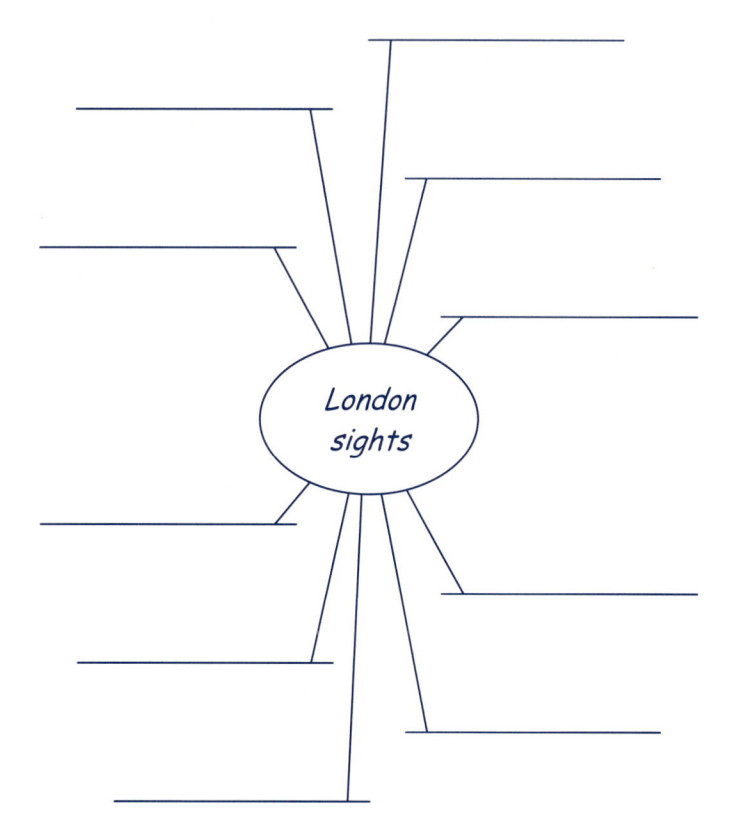

My personal list:

1 _____
2 _____
3 _____
4 _____
5 _____
6 _____
7 _____
8 _____
9 _____
10 _____

d) Write a text (60 words) about numbers 1 and 10 on your list.
Why are you interested/not interested in these sights?

*Schreibe einen Text (60 Wörter) über Nummern 1 und 10 deiner Liste.
Warum findest du diese Sehenswürdigkeiten so interessant bzw. uninteressant?*

Planning a day in London KV **1.5**

Imagine you are going on a class trip to London. You and one of your friends have to choose sights for one day. You share the work. You plan the morning and your friend plans the afternoon.

a) *Below, you can see some of the most famous London sights and the underground stations that are close by. Choose three sights for the morning.*

Unten siehst du eine Liste mit einigen der berühmtesten Sehenswürdigkeiten in London. Wähle drei für den Vormittag aus.

London sights and Tube stations

The London Eye (Waterloo station)
London Trocadero (Piccadilly Circus)
Hyde Park (Marble Arch)
Natural History Museum (South Kensington)
Brick Lane (Aldgate East)
The Gherkin (Aldgate)
St Paul's Cathedral (St. Paul's)
Buckingham Palace (St. James's Park)
Tower of London (Westminster)
Covent Garden (Covent Garden)
Leicester Square (Covent Garden)
Trafalgar Square (Charing Cross)
Tate Modern (Southwark or Blackfriars)
Madame Tussauds (Marylebone Street)
Camden (Lock) Market (Camden station)

1 _____ tube station: _____

2 _____ tube station: _____

3 _____ tube station: _____

1.5 KV Planning a day in London

b) Look at the London Tube map on p. 14 in your book and plan your trip. Take the shortest way so that you do not lose time. Your youth hostel is close to London Bridge Tube Station, so you start from there.

Schau dir den Londoner U-Bahn-Plan an und plane deinen Ausflug. Nimm den kürzesten Weg, damit du keine Zeit verlierst. Deine Jugendherberge ist in der Nähe der U-Bahnstation London Bridge, also beginnst du von dort.

Starting point: London Bridge

1   Sight: _____

    Line(s): _____

    (change at _____

    to _____ Line)

2   Sight: _____

    Line(s): _____

    (change at _____

    to _____ Line)

3   Sight: _____

    Line(s): _____

    (change at _____

    to _____ Line)

---

c) Now collect some information about the sights. What can you look at? What can you do? You can use your book if you want to. Write down the most important information. Use keywords.

Nun sammle einige Informationen über die von dir ausgewählten Sehenswürdigkeiten. Was kannst du dir genau anschauen? Was kann man dort machen? Du kannst dein Buch zur Hilfe nehmen, wenn du möchtest. Notiere Stichwörter.

d) Now write an e-mail to your friend in which you tell him/her about your plans for the morning. Explain which sights you chose, how you get to them and what you can do there.

Schreibe deinem Freund/deiner Freundin eine E-Mail, in der du ihm/ihr von deinen Plänen berichtest. Erläutere, welche Sehenswürdigkeiten du ausgewählt hast, wie man dorthin gelangt und was man dort machen kann.

Dear Pete,

I have been organizing our day in London for hours now. Here are my suggestions for the morning: we start at ...

A postcard from London KV 1.6

Dear Thomas,

I have to go now, we need to catch the bus to our youth hostel. But today was a brilliant day. We went to Madame Tussauds in the morning. We saw the London Eye just a few minutes ago. In the afternoon we were at Buckingham Palace. Madame Tussauds was very expensive. The food in the hostel is OK. I didn't see the Queen at the palaye. How is your leg? I'm sharing a room with Simon and Lukas. The bus trip here was very long, we slept on the bus. The weather is fine, so no London rain ☺. Mr Schmidt woke us at 7.30! Too early, I think. I will call you when I am back home,

Yours, Niklas

Thomas Evans
34 Owen Street
Carmarthen
SA 34 OJP Carms.
Great Britain

"That's not a good postcard for Thomas," he thinks, and buys a new one.
He wants to write a better postcard this time.

Can you help Niklas? He already knows what he wants to change:

Kannst du Niklas helfen? Er weiß schon, was er ändern möchte:

1. He wants to put the information into the right order.
2. He wants to add more linking words (after, in the morning, in the afternoon, in the evening, because, but, so, and, then, first, when, …).

Dear Thomas,

_____
_____
_____
_____
_____
_____
_____
_____
_____

Yours, Niklas

Thomas Evans
34 Owen Street
Carmarthen
SA 34 OJP Carms.
Great Britain

Unit 2 – Überblick

KV 2.1 Focus on words: Electronic media

In dieser KV sollen die S aktuelle und bereits bekannte *words and phrases* zum Thema *electronic media* (re-)aktivieren und der Situation angemessen verwenden.

KV 2.2 Focus on grammar: My diary

In dieser KV sollen die S das *present progressive* verwenden, wenn es nicht um die Gegenwart sondern um geplante Ereignisse in der Zukunft geht.

KV 2.3 Focus on grammar: What will the future be like?

Mit dieser KV wird die Verwendung des *will-future* für Vermutungen oder Vorhersagen über die Zukunft wiederholt und inhaltlich die Auseinandersetzung mit der Zukunft angestoßen.

KV 2.4 Focus on grammar: Spontaneous decisions

In dieser KV geht es um die Verwendung des *will-future* bei spontanen Entscheidungen oder Angeboten.

KV 2.5 Focus on grammar: What would you do?

In dieser KV werden Kontexte vorgegeben, die die Verwendung des *conditional II* im *if-clause*-Gefüge fordern.

KV 2.6 Proverbs and morals

In dieser KV sollen die S zur Erweiterung der Sprach- und Handlungsfähigkeit in der Zielsprache Sprichwörter kennenlernen. Bei dieser Gelegenheit werden sie dazu aufgefordert, Bedeutungen aus dem Zusammenhang zu erschließen und sie können ihre Erfahrungen im Umgang mit dem Wörterbuch vertiefen. Gleichzeitig erkennen sie Unterschiede und Gemeinsamkeiten zwischen Ziel- und Muttersprache(n).

Focus on words: Electronic media KV **2.1**

a) *Scrambled words – all the words have something to do with electronic media. Can you find the hidden words?*

All diese Wörter haben etwas mit elektronischen Medien zu tun. Kannst du die versteckten Wörter finden?

athc _____

diveso _____

onsetring _____

bilome _____

mages _____

loondawd _____

extt gasseme _____

tisesbew _____

rittnnee _____

b) *Complete the text with words from a).*

Trage die Wörter aus **a)** in die Lücken ein.

The world today is full of electronic media. If you want to tell a friend where you plan to meet him/her, just write a very short letter called _____ _____ on your _____ phone and he/she will get it in only a few seconds. If people want to have something special and not the boring "ring-ring", they get crazy _____ for their telephones. They just _____ them from _____. Almost every company, school or organization has one where you can find the information that you need.

Of course, young people use their computers for playing _____ or watching _____, too. But they also use the _____ to do their homework and prepare presentations. And they _____ as well, which is much cheaper and quicker than talking on the phone.

c) *When and why do you use electronic media in your everyday life?*

Wann und warum benutzt du elektronische Medien im Alltag?

_____

_____

_____

_____

_____

_____

2.2 KV Focus on grammar: My diary

a) This is Sarah's diary for next week. She is very busy.
Her friend Mark calls her to meet her. Can you answer for her?

Hier ist Sarahs Kalendar für die kommende Woche. Sie hat sehr viel vor.
Ihr Freund Mark ruft an, weil er sich mit ihr treffen möchte. Kannst du für sie antworten?

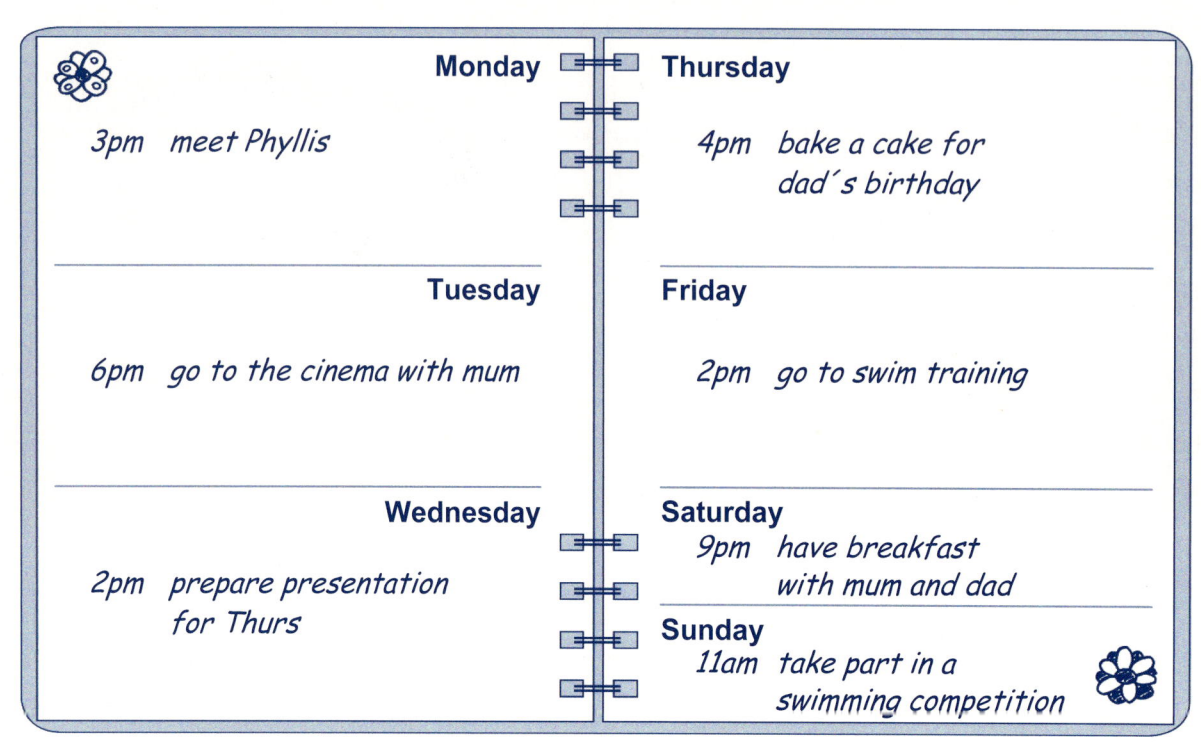

Monday
3pm   meet Phyllis

Tuesday
6pm   go to the cinema with mum

Wednesday
2pm   prepare presentation for Thurs

Thursday
4pm   bake a cake for dad's birthday

Friday
2pm   go to swim training

Saturday
9pm   have breakfast with mum and dad

Sunday
11am   take part in a swimming competition

On Sunday at 6pm, Mark calls Sarah.

Mark: Hello Sarah, how are you?

Sarah: Hey Mark! I'm doing my homework at the moment. Do you want to help me?

Mark: Haha, no! Can we meet next week? What about tomorrow afternoon?

Sarah: Sorry, I can't. *I am meeting Phyllis at 3 o'clock.* _____.

Mark: Oh, OK! What about Tuesday then?

Sarah: Well, on Tuesday _____.

Mark: Hmm. Let me think. I can meet you on Thursday. What about that?

Sarah: Thursday? No, _____.

Mark: That's very nice of you! Then let's meet on Friday.

Sarah: _____.

Mark: I have an idea, there is a brilliant market on Saturday mornings in King's Street.

Sarah: _____.

Mark: That's a pity. Then there's only Sunday left.

Sarah: _____.

Mark: OK! Then I will come with you and cheer[1] for you!

Sarah: That's a great idea! See you on Sunday then! Bye Mark!

Mark: Bye Sarah!

---
[1] anfeuern, jubeln

Focus on grammar: My diary   KV   2.2

b) 👥 *This is your diary for next week. Fill in all your plans. Your partner does the same with his/her diary. Remember not to show your diary to your partner. Then try to arrange to meet next week just like Mark and Sarah did.*

Das ist dein Kalender für die kommende Woche. Trage all deine Pläne ein. Dein Partner macht dasselbe in seinem/ihrem Kalender. Denkt aber daran, eurem Partner den ausgefüllten Kalender nicht zu zeigen. Im Anschluss daran sollt ihr in einem Dialog versuchen, eine Verabredung zu treffen, genau wie Mark und Sarah es getan haben.

Your diary:

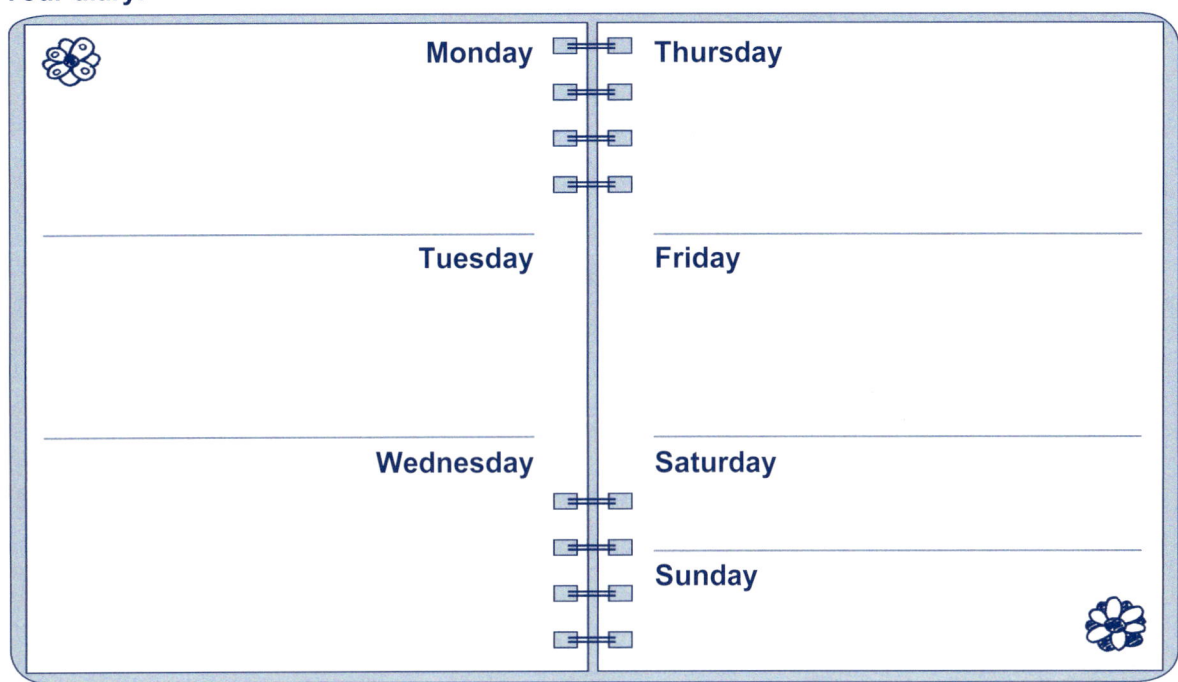

Monday	Thursday
Tuesday	Friday
Wednesday	Saturday
	Sunday

You can start your conversation like this:
Partner A: Let's meet on Thursday afternoon.
Partner B: Well, on Thursday I … But how about Tuesday?
Partner A: On Tuesday I…

c) *Now that you know what your partner is doing next week, write a text about his/her plans. You can borrow his/her diary to help you.*

Nun weißt du genau, was dein Partner nächste Woche vorhat. Schreibe einen Text über seine/ihre Pläne. Du kannst seinen/ihren Kalender zur Hilfe nehmen.

On Monday, _____

_____

_____

_____

_____

_____

_____

_____

2.3 KV Focus on grammar: What will the future be like?

a) What will life be like in the year 2525? Tick one of the boxes or describe/draw your own idea. Then make one sentence about the box you ticked.

Wie wird das Leben im Jahr 2525 aussehen? Kreuze eins der Kästchen an oder beschreibe/zeichne deine eigene Idee. Dann formuliere einen Satz zu dem ausgewählten Kästchen.

1

Example: *I don´t think there will be any trees left in the future.*

2

3

4

5

Seite 1 von 2

Focus on grammar: What will the future be like? KV 2.3

b) *Now that you've got some ideas about life in the future, write an article for your school magazine. The article must be about life in the future, but you can focus on one aspect e.g. school life, transport, food and drinks, nature, …*

Nun hast du schon einige Ideen zum Thema Leben in der Zukunft gesammelt. Schreibe einen Artikel für die Schülerzeitung, in dem es um das Leben in der Zukunft geht. Du kannst dir einen Schwerpunkt auswählen, z.B. Schulleben, Fortbewegung, Essen und Trinken, Natur, …

Remember:

Writing texts
- Before you start writing, collect ideas for your text in a network.
- When you write your text, use paragraphs.
- Start a new paragraph for each new idea.
- Start each paragraph with a topic sentence. The topic sentence gives the most important idea of the paragraph.
- Give the text a fitting title.
- Correct your text (see page 147 in your English book).

2.4 KV Focus on grammar: Spontaneous decisions

Finish the short conversations using the short form of the will-future.

Vervollständige die Kurzdialoge, indem du die Kurzformen des will-future benutzt.

1 In the Maths lesson:

- I don't understand this exercise!
- Don't worry, Pete! I'*ll help* (help) you.

2 At the local bookshop:

- Look, mum, the new Harry Potter book is out. Oh dear! I don't have enough money to buy it.
- OK, OK. I _____ (buy) it for you.

3 On the trip to France:

- Mum, dad, have we got anything left to eat? I'm so hungry!
- No, I'm sorry, Thomas, but I _____ (get) you a sandwich at the next stop.

4 At the school canteen:

- Oh, no. I forgot my purse. I can't pay for my lunch now.
- Don't worry, Jenny. I _____ (lend) you some money.

Focus on grammar: What would you do? KV 2.5

a) *Have a look at the bubbles. What would you do, feel or say in these situations?*
Schau dir die Gedankenblasen an. Was würdest du in diesen Situationen machen, fühlen oder sagen?

… was a teacher for one day

If I was a teacher for one day, I would
_____
_____

… Brad Pitt rang at my door

_____
_____

… won the lottery

_____
_____

… was a film star

_____
_____

… had an appointment with Angela Merkel

_____
_____

… lived on Hawaii

_____
_____

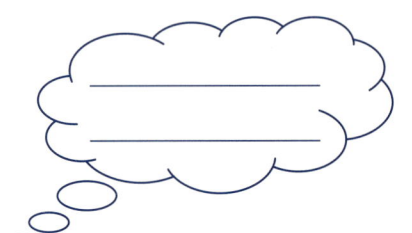

2.5 KV Focus on grammar: What would you do?

b) *Now fill in the bubbles for your partner. They can be very funny if you like. Then swap your sheets and finish the if-sentences.*

Fülle nun die Gedankenblasen für deinen Partner aus. Sie dürfen ruhig lustig werden, wenn du möchtest. Tauscht im Anschluss eure Arbeitsblätter aus und beendet die jeweiligen if-Sätze.

Remember:
Conditional Sentences (type 2)
„Was wäre, wenn ..."-Sätze: Sie drücken aus, was unter bestimmten Bedingungen sein würde, aber doch eher unwahrscheinlich ist (oder sogar unmöglich):

if-Satz (Bedingung)	Hauptsatz (Folge)
If I lived on Hawaii,	I would go surfing every day.
simple past	would + infinitive

Merke: Geht der *if*-Satz voran, werden Haupt- und Nebensatz durch ein Komma getrennt.

Proverbs: Look before you leap KV 2.6

The proverb above means that you should look at something carefully before you begin to deal with it. For example, Tina wants to spend all her money on a new pair of jeans and her best friend Jenny tells her: "Look before you leap. That's all the money you've got!" The moral is that we should be careful with a new project, especially if it is risky[1].

Here are some other English proverbs. Read them and do the following tasks for each proverb.

- **a)** Check the dictionary for unknown words.
- **b)** Think about each one and try to guess what it means.
- **c)** Is there a German equivalent? What is it?
- **d)** What is the moral of the proverb?

1 Don't put off until tomorrow what you can to today.

a) _____
b) _____
c) _____
d) _____

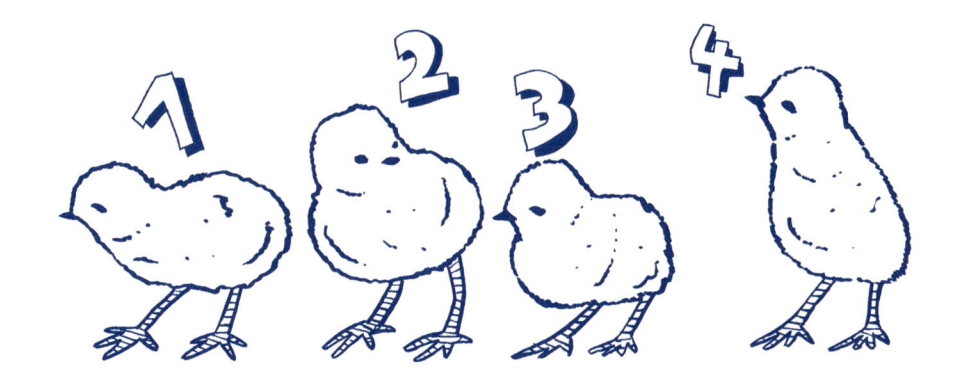

2 Don't count your chickens before they're hatched.

a) _____
b) _____
c) _____
d) _____

3 A bird in the hand is worth two in the bush.

a) _____
b) _____
c) _____
d) _____

---

[1] risky – riskant

2.6 KV Proverbs: Look before you leap

4 Don't bite the hand that feeds you.

a) _____
b) _____
c) _____
d) _____

5 Haste makes waste.

a) _____
b) _____
c) _____
d) _____

6 Too many cooks spoil the broth.

a) _____
b) _____
c) _____
d) _____

7 When life gives you lemons, make lemonade.

a) _____
b) _____
c) _____
d) _____

8 Every cloud has a silver lining.

a) _____
b) _____
c) _____
d) _____

Unit 3 – Überblick

KV 3.1 Focus on words: Sport

In dieser KV wird der Wortschatz zum Thema *sport* gefestigt und die systematische Wortfeldarbeit vertieft.

KV 3.2 Focus on grammar: Relative clauses

In dieser KV sollen die S die Verwendung der *relative pronouns* einüben und typische Verwendungssituationen von *relative clauses* kennenlernen.

KV 3.3 Focus on grammar: Contact clauses

In dieser KV sollen die S die Regeln zu den *contact clauses* erläutern. Anschließend üben sie diese anhand einer realen Anwendungssituation. Zwei Sätze werden zu einem Satz und damit stilistisch aufgewertet. Sie üben, wann sie das Relativpronomen benötigen, und wann sie es weglassen können.

KV 3.4 Focus on grammar and writing: The passive voice

In dieser KV wird die Bildung und Verwendung von Passivformen geübt, zunächst in einem Lückentext, dann in einem freien Schreibauftrag.

KV 3.5 Test your knowledge

Bei dieser KV wird die Verwendung des Passivs im *simple past* geübt und spielerisch mit einem Quiz zum Allgemeinwissen verknüpft.

KV 3.6 Writing a report on your last class trip

In dieser KV geht es um die Schulung und Vertiefung der Schreibkompetenzen der S. Sie schreiben einen Bericht über ihren letzten Klassenausflug. Im Zentrum der Aufmerksamkeit stehen die Ideensammlung anhand der W-Fragen und die anschließende geordnete Verschriftlichung.

3.1 KV Focus on words: Sport

a) *Fill in the crossword.*

Across:

2 Elfmeter, Strafstoß
5 Trainer
7 Pokal
10 Finale
11 Anhänger, Fan
13 Helm
14 Spielstand

Down:

1 Torwart, Torfrau
3 ausgleichen
4 trainieren
6 Platz
8 Badeanzug
9 Tor
12 Schiedsrichter

b) *Now put the words under the correct heading. Can you add more words?*

equipment	location	people	other
helmet			

Focus on grammar: Relative clauses KV 3.2

a) You know that an English-German Dictionary helps you when you want to find out what a word means in German. In a monolingual[1] dictionary, there are explanations for the words in English like the definitions below. Fill in the missing relative pronoun **which** or **who**.
Can you add the missing definitions?

*Ein Englisch-Deutsches Wörterbuch hilft dir, wenn du herausfinden möchtest, was ein Wort auf Deutsch heißt. In einem einsprachigen Wörterbuch findest du Erklärungen für die englischen Wörter wie die untenstehenden Definitionen. Trage die Relativpronomen ein (**who** oder **which**). Kannst du die Definitionen ergänzen?*

An elephant is an animal _____ lives in Africa and Asia.

A teacher is someone _____ works in a school.

Chalk is something _____ writes white on a blackboard.

The internet is something _____ helps you to find important information.

A map _____.

A referee _____.

A car _____.

A shop assistant _____.

b) Fill in the correct relative pronoun **who** or **which**.

*Trage die Relativpronomen ein (**who** oder **which**).*

Toby and Fiona are friends _____ have gone to school together for years. Now Toby's father, _____ works at a bank, has found a new job in Cardiff. So the Peterson family has to move. Toby, _____ likes his home town Canterbury very much, is sad. "Canterbury has got a great football team, all my friends live here – I even like my school! I don't know what I will miss most" he says angrily. So Fiona has got an idea: she wants to have a farewell party[2]. She invites the people _____ have been friends with the Petersons for years. Everybody _____ comes prepares something to eat _____ the Petersons like very much.

The evening of the party has arrived: The Petersons don't know anything about the party _____ is about to start any minute now. Fiona rings the bell and Mr Peterson, _____ looks very tired because of all the packing, opens the door. "Surprise" Fiona shouts, and all the friends _____ are invited, come round the corner. Mr Peterson calls his wife and children, _____ have been sitting in the empty living room. They can't believe it.

They now know that they will miss their friends most!

---

[1] monolingual – einsprachig
[2] farewell party - Abschiedsfeier

3.3 KV Focus on grammar: Contact clauses

a) You know relative clauses and the relative pronouns. But did you know that some relative clauses are correct without a relative pronoun?
Look at the following examples and complete the rule.

Du kennst Relativsätze und die Relativpronomen. Aber wusstest du, dass manche Relativsätze auch ohne Relativpronomen gebildet werde können? Schau dir die Beispiele an und vervollständige die Regel.

This is the boy (who) I met last week.   The dog (which) I have is old.
This is the boy who plays football.   The restaurant which opened last week is great.

> **Rule:** If *who*, *which* or *that* is the _____ of the relative clause, you can leave it out. You call these relative clauses _____ clauses.
>
> If *who*, *which* or *that* is followed by a _____, it is the _____ and you cannot leave it out!

b) Now you: Form one sentence with a relative clause from two individual sentences. Use a relative pronoun when necessary.

Und jetzt du: Bilde einen Relativsatz aus zwei Einzelsätzen und verwende das Relativpronomen, wenn es nicht weggelassen werden kann.

1 Look at Sharon's earrings. She made them herself.
   _____

2 The train is late. It arrives on platform 3.
   _____

3 There are many cars. They drive too fast.
   _____

4 We went to a concert. It took place in the concert hall.
   _____

5 London is a city. Toby loves it very much.
   _____

6 Tiger is a beautiful cat. Ella's father bought it for her.
   _____

7 We are late. This is not very nice of us.
   _____

8 I read an exciting book. My mum bought it for me.
   _____

9 You are a great friend. I like you very much.
   _____

10 Mowgli is a little boy. He lives in the jungle.
   _____

Focus on grammar and writing: The passive voice KV 3.4

a) Read the text about football and fill in the correct form of the verbs in the simple present. Use passive forms where you need them.

Lies den Text über Fußball und trage die korrekten Verbformen im Präsens ein. Benutze Passivformen, wo sie dir sinnvoll erscheinen.

Football – the greatest sport in the world

Football or soccer _____ (be) a team sport that _____ (play) between two teams of eleven players. It _____ (see) as the most popular sport in the world by many people. Football _____ (play) on a rectangular grass field with a goal at each of the short ends. The aim of the game _____ (be) to kick a ball into the opposing goal. Only the goalkeepers _____ (be allowed) to touch the ball with their hands or arms, the rest of the team normally _____ (kick) the ball with their feet. Although players usually _____ (use) their feet to move the ball around, they may _____ (touch) the ball with any part of their bodies other than their hands or arms. When the ball _____ (hit) by the player's head, it _____ (call) a header. Physical contact between the players of the opposing teams _____ (be forbidden). The referee can _____ (stop) the match when a player _____ (foul) by another one, and the match _____ (continue) after a free kick or a yellow or red card for very hard fouls. The team that _____ (score) the most goals by the end of the match _____ (win). If both teams _____ (score) an equal number of goals then the game _____ (be) a draw[1]. You _____ (play) for 90 minutes and _____ (have) a break of 15 minutes in between. After the break the teams _____ (change) sides.

b) "Football is said to be the greatest sport in the world." Do you agree with this statement? Say why or why not.

_____

_____

c) What is your favourite sport? Describe it and explain some of its most important rules. Use passive forms where they are useful.

Was ist dein Lieblingssport? Beschreibe ihn und erkläre seine wichtigsten Regeln. Benutze die Passivformen, wo sie dir sinnvoll erscheinen.

---

[1] a draw – unentschieden

3.5 KV Test your knowledge

Complete the sentences and fill in the correct form of the verbs from the box.
Use the simple past in the passive voice. Find the hidden word.

Vervollständige die Sätze mit den richtigen Verbformen. Wähle ein Verb aus der Box.
Benutze Passivformen im simple past. Finde das versteckte Wort.

> write • train • say • build • discover • win • sing • give • invent • be born

1 Shakira _____
- ☐ l) in Brazil.
- ☐ m) in Colombia.
- ☐ n) in Portugal.

2 The song *Viva la Vida* _____
- ☐ a) by Coldplay.
- ☐ b) by Oasis.
- ☐ c) by Travis.

3 Harry Potter _____
- ☐ n) by J.K. Rowling.
- ☐ o) by J.K. Powling.
- ☐ p) by J.K. Knowling.

4 At the World Cup in 2006 the German national football team _____
- ☐ a) by Jürgen Klinsmann.
- ☐ b) by Rudi Völler.
- ☐ c) by Joachim Löw.

5 The World Cup 2006 _____
- ☐ h) by Italy.
- ☐ i) by Germany.
- ☐ j) by Brazil.

6 The Gherkin _____
- ☐ d) by Frank Lloyd Wright.
- ☐ e) by Sir Norman Foster.
- ☐ f) by Frank O. Gehry.

7 The telephone _____
- ☐ q) by Werner Braun.
- ☐ r) by Arthur Gordon Pym.
- ☐ s) by Alexander Graham Bell.

8 Nessie is the name that _____ to the monster that lives
- ☐ t) in Loch Ness.
- ☐ u) in Loch Vess.
- ☐ v) Loch Lomond.

9 America _____
- ☐ d) by Vasco da Gama.
- ☐ e) by Columbus.
- ☐ f) by Alexander von Humboldt.

10 "That's one small step for a man, but a giant leap for mankind" _____
- ☐ r) by Neil Armstrong.
- ☐ s) by Yuri A. Gagarin.
- ☐ t) by Amis Strong.

Solution: __ __ __ __ __ __ __ __ __ __
         1 2 3 4 5 6 7 8 9 10

Writing a report on your last class trip KV 3.6

a) *What can you remember about your last class trip? Write a report on it for your school's year book. Start collecting information for the "5 Ws" and say how you liked the trip:*

Sicherlich kannst du dich noch an deinen letzten Klassenausflug erinnern. Schreibe darüber einen Bericht für das Jahresheft deiner Schule. Beginne damit, Informationen für die „5 Ws" zu sammeln und schreibe auf, wie dir der Ausflug gefallen hat:

questions	information	order
WHO?		
WHERE? (Where did you go? Where did you stay?)		
WHAT? (What did you do? Did you go on any day trips? Did you play any games? Did you do any sports? …)		
WHEN? (Which month? Time of the year? What was the weather like?...)		
WHY? (What was the aim/reason for your class trip?)		
HOW? (How did you like the trip? What was the atmosphere like in the group?		

b) *Now put your information in a useful order by adding numbers in the third column. Then write the report. Don't forget to link your ideas.*
When you have finished, read the text again and then find a good title for it.

Nun bringe die Informationen in eine sinnvolle Reihenfolge, indem du in der dritten Spalte Nummern ergänzt. Dann schreibe den Bericht! Vergiss nicht, deine Ideen zu verknüpfen.
Wenn der Text fertig ist, lies ihn noch einmal durch und finde eine passende Überschrift.

Here are some ideas that my help you.

> take the … / go by train, by coach
> stay at a youth hostel / camping site / hotel
> go on day / bicycle trips
> play funny games together
> stay up late
> go for a walk (in the night)
> play table tennis / basketball / football
> organize a disco
> sing together
> have a lot of fun

Unit 4 – Überblick

KV 4.1 A crossword on Canada

In dieser Wortschatz-orientierten KV wird das neu gelernte Vokabular zum Thema *Canada* gefestigt.

KV 4.2 Revision: The Passive

Bei dieser KV wird die Verwendung des Passivs wiederholend zunächst in die Thematik der aktuellen Unit eingebettet eingeübt. Im Anschluss daran erfolgt über einen Bildimpuls eine erneute Bewusstmachung für Situationen, in denen das Passiv verwendet wird.

KV 4.3 Focus on grammar: Simple past and past perfect

In dieser KV wird die Verwendung von *simple past* und *past perfect* anhand eines Lückentextes geübt. Es folgt eine Schreibübung, bei der die S einen freien Text verfassen sollen.

KV 4.4 Focus on grammar: Indirect speech

Diese KV schult die Lesekompetenz und festigt den Gebrauch der *indirect speech*.

KV 4.5 Mediation: A Telephone conversation

Bei dieser KV üben die S das sinngemäße Übersetzen – *mediation*.

KV 4.5 Writing a story

Bei dieser mehrschrittigen Schreibaufgabe werden die S mit Hilfe von Checklisten und *picture prompts* auf das Verfassen eines freien Textes vorbereitet. Dabei werden die *steps of writing* wiederholt und gefestigt.

A crossword on Canada KV 4.1

Test your knowledge on Canada and fill in the crossword.

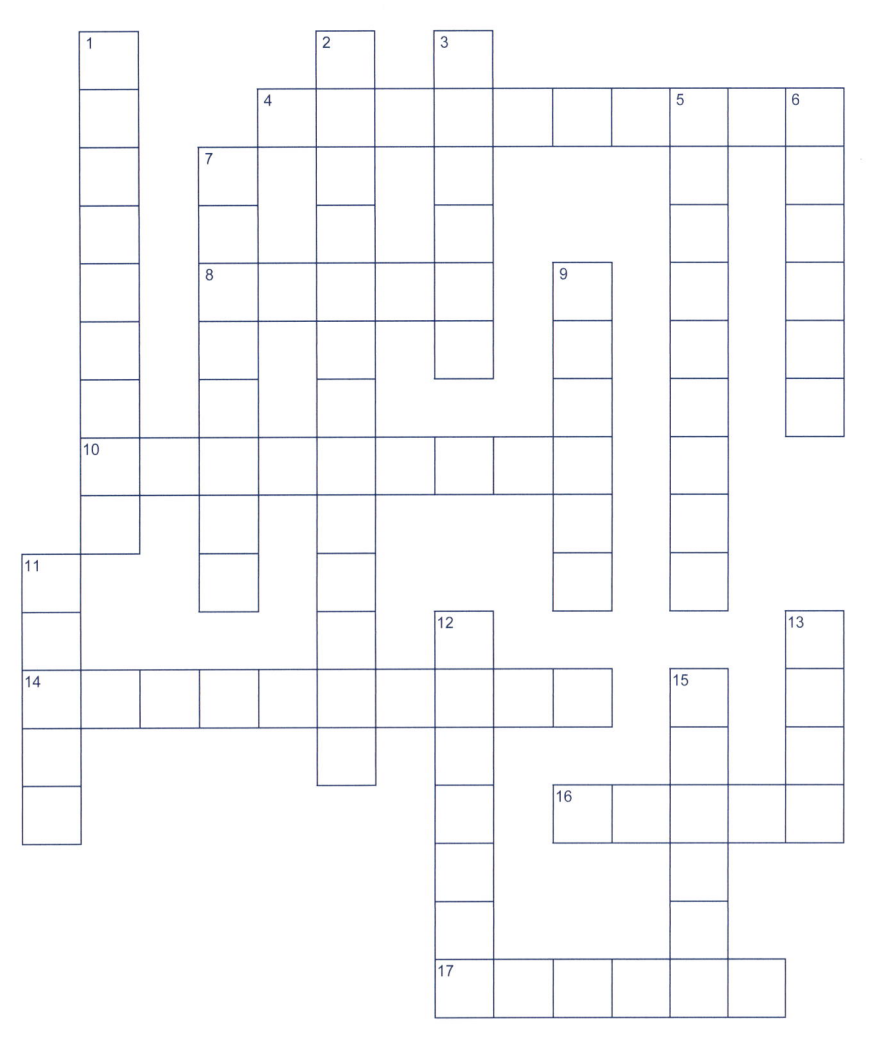

Across:
4 The city of Toronto has a ………………………… of about 2,500,000.
8 A type of boat in which you paddle.
10 Somebody who catches animals which live in rivers, lakes or the ocean.
14 A place where you can put up your tent or park your caravan.
16 The …………… people live in the coldest parts of our planet.
17 A kind of policeman for a national park.

Down:
1 Every nation has got its own ……… …… …………
2 If you work without taking money for it, you do ……………………… …………
3 A big city in Canada.
5 The Canadian national winter sport: ……… ………………
6 The people living in one country make up the ………………
7 A famous sport in Canada which only very few people in Europe know about.
9 Jacques is from Quebec, so he speaks ……………… and English.
11 You can find out what's happening in your town if you buy a …………… newspaper.
12 When you do ………………… activities you are outside a lot.
13 To kill wild animals either for food or for sport is the same as to ………… them.
15 If you describe the size of a piece of land, you use ……………… km.

4.2 KV Revision: The passive

a) You have probably seen boats before. But have you ever seen dragon boats?
They are something special, and there are lots of them in Canada. Read the following text and fill in the gaps using either the active or the passive form of the verb.

Du hast bestimmt schon einmal Boote gesehen. Aber kennst du auch Drachenboote? Sie sind etwas Besonderes, und in Kanada gibt es sehr viele davon.
Lies den folgenden Text und fülle die Lücken mit dem Aktiv oder Passiv des Verbs.

Dragon boats _____ (be) an old Chinese tradition. But they _____ (also/can find) in Canada. They _____ (be) very popular here. In Toronto, there _____ (be) 20,000 dragon boaters. Every year, a festival with many dragon boat races _____ (to organize). Dragon boats are canoes which _____ (decorate) with dragons' heads. They _____ (steer) by one person only, but there are 20 people in one boat who _____ (paddle). It is important that the crew _____ (paddle) at the same speed. In the training session, many people _____ (join) the crews. The training _____ (go on) for weeks and weeks. The race itself _____ (be) only 200m long, but it is very hard. Once the dragon boats _____ (reach) the finish line, the dragon boaters _____ (celebrate) by the audience. They _____ (clap) their hands and _____ (shout) the teams' names. Each dragon boat team _____ (have) their own fan club with posters and flags. The day of the race _____ (be) something special for everybody – for those who are paddling as well as for those who are watching.

Remember:
You often find the passive in the news, for example in newspaper articles, on signs or to express rules. The reason for this is that with the passive you can describe an action without saying who does or did it.

Revision: The passive KV **4.2**

b) The following pictures show situations that can best be described in a passive sentence. What can you see?

In den folgenden Bildern siehst du Situationen, die man am besten im Passiv beschreibt. Was siehst du?

Example: *A bicycle was stolen.*

The pizza _____

Ice hockey _____

Criminals _____

King Kong _____

Music _____

4.3 KV Focus on grammar: Simple past and past perfect

a) *Jack was on holiday in Canada. He fell in love with Anna, a girl he met there. But there was also Scott, his biggest rival[1]. Somehow, Scott always seemed to be first. Read Jack's report about his "most unlucky days" and fill in the missing verbs in the simple past, past perfect or past progressive. Sometimes you have to use passive forms.*

A few weeks ago I _____ (go) to Canada on holiday with my family. We _____ (never be) there before, so everything was exciting and new. But the most exciting moment _____ (be) when I first _____ (meet) Anna. She _____ (stay) at the same hotel. I _____ (see) her in the restaurant. Our eyes _____ (meet) but when I _____ (want) to talk to her, somebody else _____ (be) faster than me. It was Scott, who _____ (stay) at the same hotel. This _____ (be) the moment when our stupid competition _____ (begin). We _____ (start) little games to impress Anna. First, we _____ (climb) up a mountain from different starting points. When I finally _____ (get) to the top of it, Scott _____ (already arrive). Proudly, he _____ (take) photos of himself at the cross. Next, we _____ (go fishing). When I _____ (want) to show Anna the fish I _____ (catch), Scott _____ (be) already at her side with a fish twice as big as mine in his hand.

Then I _____ (have) a brilliant idea. I _____ (go) to the local cinema to buy two tickets for the latest romance with Brad Pitt. When I _____ (arrive) at the ticket office, of course, all the tickets _____ (be sold out). Guess, who _____ (get) the last two tickets? You're right, it was Scott!

The next morning I _____ (buy) a nice bunch[2] of flowers for Anna. I _____ (knock) at her door and when she _____ (open) it, somebody else _____ (already give) her a massive bunch of red roses. Yuck! That _____ (be) the moment when I _____ (decide) to stop that ridiculous[3] game. I _____ (have) a nice day. I _____ (go swimming), _____ (sleep) in the sun and in the evening I _____ (make) a fire, which I _____ (collect) some wood for in the afternoon. When I _____ (sit) by the fire, suddenly somebody _____ (sit down) next to me. It _____ (be) Anna. She _____ (take) my hand, _____ (smile) at me and we _____ (have) a wonderful evening. We _____ (spend) the rest of the time together. Scott _____ (be quickly forgotten) …

---

[1] rival – Rivale, Gegner
[2] bunch – Strauß
[3] ridiculous – lächerlich

Focus on grammar: Simple past and past perfect — KV 4.3

b) *Now you. Have a look at the pictures and write the report from either Anna's or Scott's perspective.*

4.4 KV Focus on grammar: Indirect speech

Tina and Sally are best friends. They do everything together – almost everything! Tina broke her leg two weeks ago and has to stay at home now. So Sally went to Frank's party alone. But of course Tina wants to know everything about the party. Who was there? Which music was played? What was the room like? …

Sally visits Tina at home and they talk about the party:

Sally: Hello Tina, how are you?

Tina: Hey Sally, how are you? You look tired. When did you come back from the party?

Sally: My mum picked me up at Frank's house at 10.30 pm. But I didn't sleep well.

Tina: What's wrong?

Sally: Well, you know that I was at Frank's party. And you know that I like him a lot. I mean I really like him!

Tina: I know, you really really like him Sally, go on!

Sally: There were these two girls from Langton Grammar School. They are in Frank's tennis team. And I think one of them likes him, too!

Tina: Oh no, how do you know? Did they tell you anything about it?

Sally: Of course not. But I listened to them when they were talking to each other in the kitchen.

Tina: What did they say? And I want all the details, Sally!

Sally: OK, OK. Well…

This is what Sally heard in the kitchen yesterday. Put the sentences into reported speech like Sally does when she tells Tina about it.

Jennifer: Did you see Frank?

Jennifer wanted to know if _____

Amber: Of course. He is talking to that girl all Sally the time.

Amber said that _____

Jennifer: Is she one of his classmates from Barrington Grammar School?

_____

Amber: Yes, she is. She was Miss Barrington last year.

_____

Focus on grammar: Indirect speech KV 4.4

Jennifer: She looks good. Do you think she will ask Frank out on a date?

_____

Amber: No, she has got a boyfriend, his name is Fred.

_____

Jennifer: That's Tina's boyfriend, Sally's best friend.

_____

Amber: Oh no. Then I am going to ask him out. Now!

_____

Jennifer: That's a good idea. But let us have one of those sausages first.

_____

Amber: Oh, OK … Did you hear that? The door is shut. Oh no, we can't get out of the kitchen! Somebody locked us here! Help!!!

Jennifer: Well, don't panic. At least we've got enough to eat here. Hihihi!

Back in the girls' room …

Tina: Sally, you didn't, did you?

Sally: Of course! I locked the two girls in the kitchen. Then I met Frank, asked him out and we are meeting tonight. Now you know why I didn't sleep well last night.

Tina: Oh Sally, I am so proud of you. Well done, and good luck for tonight. Now, what are you going to wear?

4.5 KV Mediation: A telephone conversation

Simon and Stefan are best friends, but Simon lives in Bradford and Stefan in Hamburg. Since they don't see each other very often they write e-mails a lot. But today, Simon can't go online, so he calls Stefan. Of course, he is nervous. When they write, he has time to think about the words and sentences he writes or to look up words in the dictionary, but on the phone he needs to say everything very quickly.

Can you help him? Translate what Stefan wants to say.

Remember:
- Übersetze nicht alles wörtlich, sondern gib den Sinn wieder.
- Gib nur das Wesentliche weiter, lass Unwichtiges weg.
- Verwende kurze und einfache Sätze.
- Wenn du ein Wort nicht kennst, umschreibe es oder ersetze es durch ein anderes Wort.

Stefan: Stefan Schmidt.
Simon: Hello Stefan, this is Simon from Bradford. How are you?
Stefan: Simon? Äh… Hello!
Simon: My computer isn't working and I can't e-mail you, so I thought I'd give you a call.
Stefan: Oh, your computer, yes, äh… ach so!
Simon: Sorry, what did you say?
Stefan: (Sage, dass du dich freust, von Simon zu hören.)

_____

Simon: Yes, ist' nice to talk to you too. What are you doing at the moment?
Stefan: (Sage, dass du gerade Computer spielst und frage Simon, was er gerade tut.)

_____

Simon: Well, I am calling you, no, I was just joking, I have been watching TV, but nothing interesting was on. What do you usually watch on TV, Stefan?
Stefan: (Sage, dass du gerne Quizsendungen siehst. Deine Lieblingsshow ist *Wer wird Millionär*.)

_____

Simon: Oh I know that one! In England it's called Who wants to be a millionaire. I like it, too. There is nothing else to do at the moment but watch TV, because it's raining outside. What's the weather like in Hamburg?
Stefan: (Sage, dass gerade die Sonne scheint und dass du heute mit dem Fahrrad einen Ausflug zum Hafen gemacht hast.)

_____

_____

Simon: That sounds nice! I should come to Germany and visit you. Where exactly is Hamburg, Stefan?
Stefan: (Sage, dass Hamburg eine Stadt in Norddeutschland ist und ca. 1 800 000 Einwohner hat.)

_____

Mediation: A telephone conversation KV 4.5

Simon: That sounds nice! What can you do in Hamburg? Are there any famous sights I should visit?
Stefan: (Sage, dass Hamburg am Wasser liegt und man eine Bootstour durch den Hafen machen kann.)

_____

Simon: And what can we do in the evenings?
Stefan: (Sage, dass man sich viele verschiedene Musicals anschauen kann, aber auch Rockkonzerte.)

_____

Simon: What about Coldplay? Do they have a show in Hamburg, too? I really like them. What's your favourite band?
Stefan: (Sage, dass du auch gerne Coldplay hörst, aber auch die Red Hot Chili Peppers.)

_____

Simon: Yes, they are great! Well, Stefan, it was nice talking to you. Maybe we should talk to each other on the phone more often. Would you like to call me some time?
Stefan: (Sage, dass es für dich auch schön war, mit ihm zu telefonieren. Du hoffst, dass er dich verstehen konnte, da du es nicht gewöhnt seist, am Telefon Englisch zu sprechen.)

_____

_____

Simon: I understood you perfectly well, Stefan, don't worry. But sometimes even people from England don't understand me because of my accent, so I know what you're talking about.
Stefan: (Sage, dass du ihn gut verstanden hast. Frage ihn, ob du ihn vor deiner nächsten Englischarbeit anrufen könntest, um mit ihm die indirekte Rede zu wiederholen.)

_____

_____

Simon: Of course, and I will call you before my next German test. I am already very nervous about it. Goodbye and take care!
Stefan: Goodbye, Simon, and thanks for calling me!

Stefan hangs up the phone and says: Puh, geschafft, Mann war das aufregend!

4.6 KV Writing a story

a) Put the writing steps into the correct order.

☐ Structure your ideas in a mind map or a chart (use the 5 'W's and 'How').

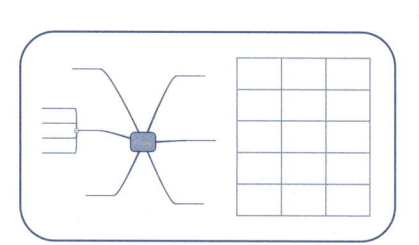

☐ Brainstorm ideas.

☐ Write the story in three parts: a beginning, a middle part and an end.

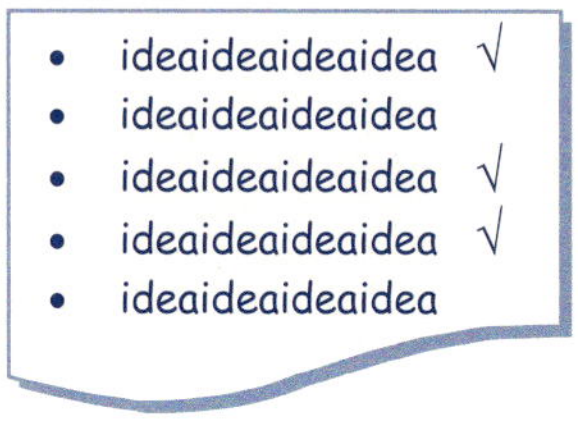

☐ Choose the best ideas.

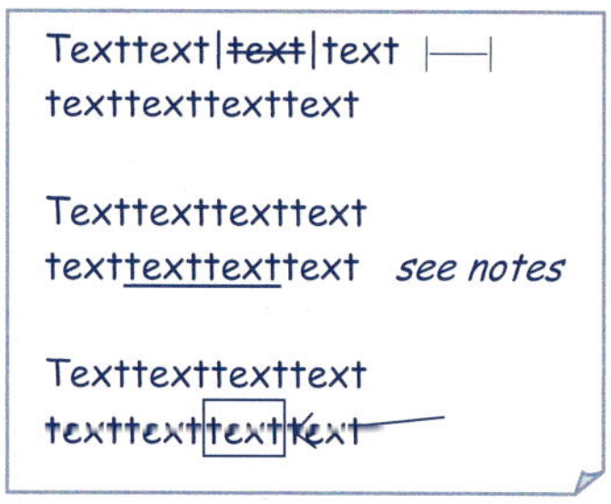

☐ Revise the story (read it, check for mistakes and correct them).

☐ Write down <u>every</u> idea.

b) Look at the pictures. They show you the beginning of a story. How might the story continue? Brainstorm ideas and follow the writing steps.

Writing a story KV 4.6

You can start like this or find your own beginning for the story.

Jeremy was alone on a very stormy night. His parents had gone to see some friends who lived about 20 miles away. After he had watched some television, Jeremy went to bed and fell asleep. He was dreaming about the film he had watched, but now **he** was the hero who saved the lives of the people who had been kidnapped … Suddenly he was woken up by very loud thunder. He wanted to switch the light on, but it didn't work. So he took a torch[1] and went down into the cellar where his father always went when there was no electricity. He went slowly down the stairs and then 'krk', 'krk', 'krk' …

_____
_____
_____
_____
_____
_____
_____
_____
_____
_____

c) *After you have written the story check the following:*

Have you …
- found a good title for your story?
- used adjectives and adverbs to make your story more lively?
- used linking words and time phrases?
- checked the spelling?
- checked for mistakes (verb forms, word order)?
- checked the order of events? Is it clear?
- divided your text into a beginning, a middle and an end? Are there clear paragraphs?

Well done! You are a good story writer!

_____

[1] torch – Taschenlampe

Unit 5 – Überblick

KV 5.1 Focus on words: Music, stars and instruments

In dieser KV üben die S zunächst die Begriffe zu den oben genannten Themen ein und verwenden diese dann in einem selbst verfassten Text, sodass auch Schreibkompetenz und Kreativität geübt werden.

KV 5.2 Talking about oneself – my own biography

In dieser KV schreiben die S im Unterschied zu den Biographien des Schülerbuches eine eigene Biographie. Das Sprechen über sich selbst ist für den kommunikativen Aspekt des Sprachenlernens ein wichtiges Element, da dies im Alltag häufig vorkommt. Die Regeln zur Textgestaltung geben Hinweise für die Überarbeitung des eigenen Textes.

KV 5.3 Focus on grammar: Reflexive pronouns and verbs

In dieser KV üben die S die *modals* und ihre Ersatzformen in einem relativ freien Text, den sie nur auf Basis von Notizen verfassen müssen. Dies ist im Vergleich zu den Übungen aus Klasse 6 eine stärker zieltextsprachliche Übung, da gleichzeitig Textgestaltung und Grammatik beachtet werden müssen.

KV 5.4 Modal substitutes: Can, must and may

Die Verwendung der *modal substitutes* wird zunächst an einem Lückentext und dann an einem von den S selbst zu verfassenden Text geübt.

KV 5.5 Focus on grammar: Conditional III

Bei dieser KV geht es gezielt um das Üben von Konditionalgefügen des dritten Typs. Außerdem werden sowohl Lese- als auch Schreibkompetenz geschult.

KV 5.6 Writing about a star

Bei dieser KV wird zunächst das Formulieren von Fragen geübt. In einem zweiten Schritt wird ausgehend von einem Interview ein zusammenhängender Text verfasst.

Focus on words: Music, stars and instruments KV **5.1**

a) Find 10 words on music, stars and instruments.

A	C	A	R	E	E	R	B	X	S
L	S	E	M	F	I	E	I	S	L
N	E	T	R	A	C	K	O	T	O
C	L	A	S	S	I	C	G	E	H
H	C	S	D	K	P	A	R	R	E
P	E	V	R	Q	O	L	A	E	O
P	O	P	U	L	P	R	P	O	V
O	L	D	M	I	S	W	H	O	S
S	S	I	S	K	T	R	Y	E	O
K	T	F	T	M	A	I	L	A	P
T	R	R	I	L	T	N	P	R	E
P	I	T	C	W	I	S	I	T	R
L	N	P	K	B	O	E	P	C	A
E	G	Z	S	N	N	U	E	M	T

b) Write down the words on the lines below.

_____

_____

c) The words you found belong to similar word fields. Write a small text with at least six of the words from the grid. The sentences have to form a proper text.

Die Wörter, die du gefunden hast, stammen aus ähnlichen Wortfeldern. Schreibe einen kleinen Text mit mindestens sechs Begriffen des Rätsels. Die Sätze sollen einen zusammenhängenden Text bilden.

5.2 KV Talking about oneself – my own biography

During the course of this unit, you have read and written various biographies of famous people. But did you ever think of writing one about your own life? There are probably a lot of things you can say about yourself even though you are not famous (yet ☺).

a) Please fill in this questionnaire to collect first ideas for writing your biography.

Fülle den Fragebogen aus, um erste Ideen zu sammeln, sodass du auf das Verfassen deiner Biographie vorbereitet bist.

Name: _____

Born (when/where): _____

Details about your family

– brothers and sisters, parents: _____
_____

– their ages, jobs, interests: _____
_____

School

– name and place: _____

– classmates and teachers: _____
_____

Hobbies: _____

---

b) Now write a proper biography. Write it on an extra piece of paper and decorate it with photos or drawings.

Schreibe nun eine vollständige Biographie. Schreibe auf einem Extrablatt und dekoriere sie mit Fotos oder Zeichnungen.

c) Use this checklist from your English book to improve your text.

- Is there a paragraph for each new idea?
- Are some sentences too short? Are there enough linking words?
- Would more adjectives or adverbs improve the text?
- Are the beginning and ending interesting?
- Will the rest interest the reader?
- Is there anything that you don't need?
- Have you got any other ideas?

Focus on grammar: Reflexive pronouns and verbs   KV 5.3

a) Complete the list of reflexive pronouns.

myself	(ich) mir	ourselves	(wir) uns
yourself	(du) dir/dich	_____	(ihr) euch
_____	(er) sich	_____	(sie) sich
_____	(sie) sich		
_____	(er/sie/es) sich		

b) Look at the pictures and add the correct reflexive pronouns to the sentences.

1 Steven taught _____ how to play the guitar.

2 Mrs Miller bought a nice bunch of flowers for _____.

3 You don't have to wash cats. They wash _____.

4 "Mum and dad are out. So we cooked _____ a nice meal."

5 "Don't look at your neighbour's test! Think for _____!"

6 "Oh dear. Nobody is answering the phone. So I'll have to talk to _____."

Seite 1 von 2

5.3 KV Focus on grammar: Reflexive pronouns and verbs

c) You know that some German verbs which need a reflexive pronoun do not need one in English, e.g. **to get dressed** – **sich anziehen**. Find all those verbs in the word snake and translate them into German.

*Du weißt, dass es im Englischen Verben gibt, die kein Reflexivpronomen bei sich führen, obwohl das Verb im Deutschen ein Reflexivpronomen verlangt, z.B. **sich anziehen** – **to get dressed**. Finde alle diese Verben in der Wortschlange und übersetze sie ins Deutsche.*

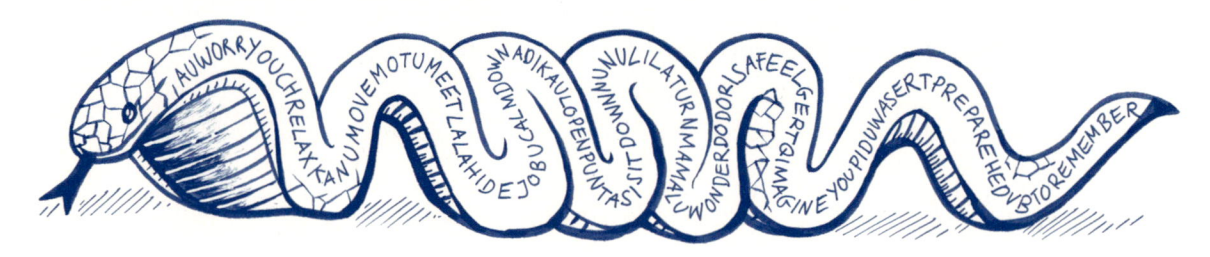

to worry – sich Sorgen machen

---

d) Complete the sentences. Decide if you need a reflexive pronoun or not.

The Weirdo family

The Weirdos are a normal family, at least that is what they think about _____.
But, dear reader, decide for _____. Emily and Jonathan Weirdo got married
13 years ago and decided to buy _____ a pink house with yellow stripes. They have
lived in it until now. They have three children: Ken, 12, who has taught _____ to
walk on his hands and turn _____ at the same time, Lisa, 10, who gets dressed
_____ in the morning with her eyes closed and little Chris, 6, who always moves
_____ in slow motion.
Every morning they meet _____ for breakfast in the kitchen and sit
_____ down under the kitchen table. Then they get _____ ready
for school or work. At school, the teachers don't worry _____ about the strange
behaviour of the kids any more and accept them the way they are. As both parents work during the day,
the kids have to cook for _____. Luckily, they never argue
_____ and live a weird, but happy life.

Modal substitutes: Can, must and may KV 5.4

Josh and Lisa bought tickets for their favourite band "The Wolves" who are playing in their town tonight. While they are waiting in front of the concert hall they look at a big sign at the entrance.

> Dear guests,
> Don't take any cameras or mobile phones inside!
> Don't take any glass bottles or alcohol inside!
> Show your tickets at the entrance!
> Show your bags to the security guard at the entrance!
> Toilets are open in the hall at all times.
> Drinks and snacks are offered at the bar.

a) Josh and Lisa are on their way into the concert hall. Fill the gaps with **can, must** or **may not**.

*Josh und Lisa sind auf dem Weg in die Konzerthalle. Vervollständige die Lücken mit **can, must** oder **may not**.*

Josh: Lisa, remember, you _____ show your ticket soon, so take it out now.

Lisa: Right, Josh, but … oh no! I forgot to take out the orange juice I bought on the way. I _____ show my bag to the security guard now and I think you _____ take glass bottles inside.

Josh: Oh – but that's no problem. Look, there is a bottle bank over there. Oh dear, I need to go to the toilet, I hope there are some inside.

Lisa: Yes, you _____ go to the toilets in the hall, no problem. Do you mind if we have a sandwich before the concert starts? I am hungry and I think there's a bar inside, where you _____ eat something.

Josh: Of course, Lisa. (*ringring*) Oops – my mobile, it's still on. I _____ switch it off, otherwise I _____ take it inside with me.

Lisa: That's right, Josh, that's why I left my camera at home, people _____ take photos of the band during concerts. And that's very sad, because I would love to have a photo of Gerry from "The Wolves" and me …

Josh: Dream on, Lisa!

5.4 KV Modal substitutes: Can, must and may

b) It's Monday morning and Josh and Lisa are talking to their friends about the weekend. They want to know everything about the "Wolves" concert. Some of them have never been to a concert before, so Lisa and Josh also tell them what you have to remember when going to a concert. Report about it and remember to use the modal substitutes for **can, may** and **must** appropriately in the simple past. There are some memories Lisa and Josh have about the concert that can help you.

*Es ist Montagmorgen und Josh und Lisa sprechen mit ihren Freunden über das Wochenende. Sie wollen alles über das Konzert der „Wolves" wissen. Viele waren noch nie auf einem Konzert, daher müssen Lisa und Josh auch berichten, was man bei einem Konzertbesuch beachten muss. Berichte über das Konzert und verwende die Ersatzformen für **can, may** und **must**, um dich in der Vergangenheit angemessen ausdrücken zu können. Unten sind ein paar Erinnerungen von Josh und Lisa an das Konzert, die dir helfen werden.*

- band cannot start before 9 pm because of technical problems
- they play all the songs and the fans sing all the texts
- Gerry sees Lisa and waves to her, but Lisa may not come up on stage
- Josh has to go to the toilet again, so he misses his favourite song
- Lisa cannot buy a T-Shirt of "The Wolves", because it's too expensive
- Technicians have to switch on the lights, when a cracker explodes in the back
- "The Wolves" can show everybody how good they are

_____
_____
_____
_____
_____
_____

Focus on grammar: Conditional III KV 5.5

a) *Match the sentence halves.*

1. If Neil Armstrong hadn't been the first man on the moon
2. If Sheila had won in the last week's lottery
3. If I hadn't played computer games the whole weekend
4. If Matthew had learned for the last class test
5. If Romeo hadn't met Juliet

a) she would have started a trip around the world.
b) his result would have been better.
c) he wouldn't have said: "It's one small step for a man, but a giant leap for mankind."
d) they would have lived longer.
e) I would have been able to go on a bike tour with my friends.

b) *Read about Sarah's dream and finish the story. Write at least five more sentences.*

Last night Sarah had a wonderful dream. She dreamt about meeting a fairy[1] who said to her: "Tell me your greatest wish and it will come true." Sarah answered: "I would like to travel to Hollywood and become a star." One minute later Sarah was on a plane to the USA. On the plane she talked to a nice boy whose name was Jeff. She enjoyed the flight and when they had to say goodbye to each other Sarah was a little bit sad. But she soon forgot about Jeff because on her first day in Hollywood she was allowed to have a look at the studios where a new film by Steven Spielberg was produced. Everything was very exciting and interesting, but the greatest thing was that Steven Spielberg started talking to her. He was very nice and answered all of Sarah's questions about the film business. At the end Spielberg asked Sarah if she wanted to play a part in his new film. She couldn't believe it – of course she wanted to. So after the rehearsals he offered her one of the main parts in his new film. She should play the young and pretty daughter of a busy couple who didn't care about her. Guess who was playing her parents: Brad Pitt was her father and Kate Winslet was her mother. During the breaks she talked to the stars and was even invited to their homes. The film became a great success and Sarah won an Oscar for her role in the film. It was absolutely fantastic. She had made it. When she was standing on the stage with the Oscar in her hand she rrrrrrrrrrrrrrrrrriiiiiiiiiiiiiiiiiiiiiiinnnnnnnnnnnnnnnggg. Her alarm clock went off. She woke up and it was a strange feeling at first. She was a little bit confused, but then she got up, had breakfast and went to school. "Damn, she thought. It was only a dream." Lessons were boring, but suddenly somebody knocked at their door. It was the headmaster of her school, but he wasn't alone. With him was a handsome American guy from Hollywood called Jeff …

---

[1] Fairy – Fee

5.5 KV Focus on grammar: Conditional III

_____
_____
_____
_____
_____
_____

c) *Now finish the following if-clauses.*

1 If Sarah hadn't met a fairy in her dream, she wouldn't have flown to Hollywood.

2 If she hadn't gone to Hollywood, she _____.

3 If she hadn't met Steven Spielberg, _____.

4 If Spielberg hadn't offered her a part in his film, _____.

5 If Sarah hadn't met Brad Pitt and Kate Winslet, _____.

6 If the film hadn't been a great success, _____.

7 If the alarm clock hadn't gone off, _____.

8 If she hadn't gone to the school that day, _____.

9 _____.

10 _____.

11 _____.

Writing about a star KV 5.6

a) *Read the interview with Lady GaGa. Write down the missing questions.*

Reporter: Hello, _____?

Lady GaGa: Fine, thank you.

Reporter: Great. So let's start with the questions.
_____?

Lady GaGa: My real name is Stefani Joanne Angelina Germanotta.

Reporter: Oh, that sounds Italian. _____?

Lady GaGa: No, I'm not from Italy. I'm from Yonkers, New York in the USA. But my parents are Italian Americans.

Reporter: _____?

Lady GaGa: I'm 23 and I was born on 23rd March 1986.

Reporter: _____?

Lady GaGa: I'm a singer, but I have also written songs for stars like Fergie, The Pussycat Dolls, Britney Spears and others.

Reporter: _____?

Lady GaGa: My first album was called *The Fame*.

Reporter: _____?

Lady GaGa: My greatest hits are "Just Dance" and "Poker Face".

Reporter: _____?

Lady GaGa: Yes, I learned to play the piano at the age of four.

Reporter: _____?

Lady GaGa: I was 13 when I wrote my first song.

Reporter: _____?

Lady GaGa: One of my best friends is Lady Starlight.

Reporter: Thanks for the interview. If your fans want to find out more about you, _____?

Lady GaGa: They can go to my official website, www.ladyGaGa.com.

Reporter: Great. Thank you and bye.

Lady GaGa: Bye.

b) *Now use the information from the interview to write a short biography of Lady GaGa.
If you need more information you can do some research on the internet.
Don't forget to check your text when you have finished!*

Benutze nun die Informationen aus dem Interview, um eine kurze Biographie über Lady GaGa zu schreiben. Wenn du mehr Informationen brauchst, recherchiere im Internet. Vergiss nicht, deinen Text zu überprüfen, wenn du fertig bist.

Lösungen

Welcome

0.1 Welcome back!
Individuelle Lösungen.

Unit 1

1.1 Town and transport

a)

Crossword:
1. CHURCH
2. UNDERGROUND
3. CINEMA
4. TAXI
5. TRAIN
6. TRAM
7. HOSPITAL
8. AIRPORT
9. FERRY
10. PLANE
11. BUS
12. HOTEL
13. STATION

b)

(to) take	the bus, the train, the underground, a taxi, the plane, the ferry
(to) wait for	the bus, the train, the underground, a taxi, the plane, the ferry
(to) wait at	the cinema, the station, the hospital, the hotel
(to) get on / off	the bus, the train, the underground, the plane, the ferry
(to) go to	the station, church, the hotel
(to) buy	a/the ticket
(to) pay for	a/the ticket, a taxi, the hotel, the ferry, the underground, …
(to) be at	the station, the hotel, the cinema, church
(to) watch	planes, trains, …

c)

1. Many people **go to church** on Sundays.
2. Let's **take the train** to London, not the bus.
3. Many years ago there were still **trams** in London. Now there are only buses and the tube.
4. Tony fell off his bike. After that he **was in hospital** for a week.
5. There's a regular **ferry** service between Oostende and Dover.
6. Trains from Brighton go to Victoria **station** in London.
7. Let's **go to the cinema** and watch a good film.
8. You can **buy tickets** at the ticket machine.
9. Heathrow is a big **airport** near London.
10. Let's go to the airport and **watch/look at planes**.
11. Come on, Peter, we have to **get off the bus** at the next stop.

1.2 Toby's homework

a)

to write	wrote	written	schreiben
to stand	stood	stood	stehen, sich (hin)stellen
to sing	sang	sung	singen
to ring	rang	rung	klingeln, läuten
to ride	rode	ridden	reiten, (Rad) fahren
to find	found	found	finden
to eat	ate	eaten	essen
to buy	bought	bought	kaufen
to give	gave	given	geben
to pay	paid	paid	bezahlen
to write	wrote	written	schreiben
to drink	drank	drunk	trinken
to teach	taught	taught	unterrichten, lehren
to bring	brought	brought	(mit-, her)bringen
to do	did	done	tun, machen

b)

1 What have you already done today?
  1 I have already **eaten** my sandwich.
  2 We have already **written** an essay in English.
  3 The pupils have already **sung** in the music lesson.

2 What haven't you done yet?
  1 I haven't **done** my homework yet.
  2 We haven't **drunk** our tea yet.
  3 My best friend hasn't **ridden** her horse yet.

3 What did you do yesterday?
  1 I **took** the books to the library.
  2 We **gave** the dogs their food.
  3 My sister **rang** her best friend on her mobile phone.

4 What didn't you do yesterday?
  1 I really didn't **eat** your chocolate!
  2 Simon didn't **pay** for lunch at school.
  3 Our teacher didn't **give** us any homework.

c)/d)

Box 1+2: **present perfect (simple)**

  ever, often, always, already, never, not ... yet, just

Box 3+4: **simple past**

  yesterday, last year, in 1989, last weekend, a week ago

1.3 Since when and for how long?
a) + b)
  Jeweils beim Partner abzulesen.

c)
  1 Mary has done judo **since** 2006.
  2 Mary has collected stamps **for** four months.
  3 Chris has played an instrument **for** three years.
  4 Thomas has done judo **since** January 2007.
  5 He has been a member in a local computer club **for** one year.
  6 Nick has done judo **since** last summer.
  7 He has been a member in a local computer club **for** eight months.

d) Anna has been waiting for the bus for 10 minutes. Tim has been talking on the phone since 2.30 pm / for half an hour. Jo and Paul have been playing football for 45 minutes / since 2.15 pm. Kim has been listening to music since 2.30 pm / for half an hour. Mr Harvey and Mrs Keitel have been talking to each other for 15 minutes / since 2.45 pm. Mrs Jones has been eating her hamburger since 2.55 pm / for five minutes.

1.4 London sights
a) Individuelle Lösungen wie z.B.:
Madame Tussauds: The queen of wax, Wax figures from yesterday and today, Men made of wax, A French wax artist, …
Camden Market: 24/7 Market with tradition, Anything every day, Shoppers' paradise, only tradition is not for sale, …

b) **T** = True / **F** = False
  1 Madame Tussaud was originally from France. **T**
  2 Madame Tussaud went to America in 1802. **F**
    Madame Tussaud went to England in 1802.
  3 There are wax museums in 10 other cities, too. **F**
    There are wax museums in 8 other cities, too.
  4 Today, there are wax figures of famous animals, too. **F**
    There are only wax figures of famous people (from the present and the past).
  5 Camden Market is a famous London fish market. **F**
    Camden Market is a London market where you can get anything.
  6 You can't buy things there on Sundays. **F**
    You can get anything there every day of the week.
  7 In the evening, you can go to restaurants, too. **T**

c) Individuelle Reihenfolge von Lösungen.
Den S bekannte Sehenswürdigkeiten in London: The London Eye, London Trocadero, Hyde Park, The Science Museum, Brick Lane, The Gherkin, St Paul's Cathedral, Buckingham Palace, Tower Bridge, Covent Garden, Leicester Square, Trafalgar Square, Nelson's Column, National Gallery, Hyde Park, South Bank, Westminster Bridge, Tate Modern, Millenium Bridge, National History Museum, Madame Tussauds, Camden (Lock) Market

d) Individuelle Lösungen.

1.5 Planning a day in London
Individuelle Lösungen.

1.6 A postcard from London
Mehrere Lösungen sind denkbar, etwa:

Dear Thomas,

How is your leg?
The bus trip here was very long, we slept in the bus. I share a room with Simon and Lukas and the food in the hostel is ok.
This morning, Mr. Schmidt woke us up at 7.30! Too early, I think. **First**, we went to Madame Tussauds. It was very expensive. **In the afternoon** we were at Buckingham Palace, **but** I didn't see the Queen. **A few minutes ago**, we saw the London eye. It was a brilliant day **because** the weather is fine, **so** no London rain ☺
I have to go now, we need to catch the bus to our youth hostel.
I will call you, when I am back home,

Yours, Niklas

Unit 2

2.1 Focus on words: Electronic media
a) chat, videos, ringtones, mobile, games, download, text message, websites, internet

b) The world today is full of electronic media. If you want to tell your friend where you want to meet him/her, you just write a very short letter called **text message** on your **mobile** phone and he/she will get it in only a few seconds. If people want to have something special and not the boring "ring-ring", they get crazy **ringtones** for their telephones. They just **download** them from **websites**. Almost every company, school or organization has got one where you can find the information that you need.
Of course, young people use their computers for playing **games** or watching **videos**, too. But they also use the **internet** to do their homework and prepare presentations. And they **chat** as well, which is much cheaper and quicker than talking on the phone.

c) Individuelle Lösungen.

2.2 Focus on grammar: My diary
a) *Sunday, 6 p.m. Mark calls Sarah.*
Mark: Hello Sarah, how are you?
Sarah: Hey Mark! I'm doing my homework at the moment. Do you want to help me?
Mark: Haha, no! I want to meet you next week. What about tomorrow afternoon?
Sarah: Sorry, I can't. **I am meeting Phyllis at 3 o'clock.** (example)
Mark: Oh, OK! What about Tuesday then?
Sarah: Well, on Tuesday **I am going to the cinema with my mum.**
Mark: Hmm. Let me think. I can meet you on Thursday. What about that?
Sarah: Thursday? No, **I am baking a cake for my dad's birthday.**
Mark: That's very nice of you! Then let's meet on Friday.
Sarah: On Friday I am going to swim training.
Mark: I have an idea, there is a brilliant market on Saturday mornings in King's street.
Sarah: On Saturday I am having breakfast with my mum and dad.
Mark: That's a pity. Then there's only Sunday left.
Sarah: On Sunday I am taking part in a swimming competition.
Mark: OK! Then I will come with you and cheer for you!
Sarah: That's a great idea! See you on Sunday then! Bye Mark!
Mark: Bye Sarah!

b) Individuelle Lösungen.

c) Individuelle Lösungen.

2.3 Focus on grammar: What will the future be like?
Individuelle Lösungen.

2.4 Focus on grammar: Spontaneous decisions
2. **I'll buy** it for you. 3. **I'll get** you a sandwich at the next stop. 4. **I'll lend** you some money.

2.5 Focus on grammar: What would you do?
a) Individuelle Lösungen.

b) Individuelle Lösungen.

2.6 Proverbs and morals

1. **Don't put off until tomorrow what you can do today.**
   a) Individuelle Lösung.
   b) to put something off – etwas aufschieben
   c) Was du heute kannst besorgen, das verschiebe nicht auf morgen.
   d) Do the things you need to do as soon as possible, don't wait too long.

2. **Don't count your chickens until they're hatched.**
   a) Individuelle Lösung.
   b) to hatch – wenn ein Vogel, Insekt oder anderes Lebewesen aus dem Ei schlüpft
   c) Lobe den Tag nicht vor dem Abend.
   d) Don't be happy about what you have done when you haven't finished yet.

3. **A bird in the hand is worth two in the bush.**
   a) Individuelle Lösung.
   b) bush – Busch
   c) Lieber den Spatz in der Hand als die Taube auf dem Dach.
   d) Be happy with what you've got and don't dream about the things that you don't have.

4. **Don't bite the hand that feeds you.**
   a) Individuelle Lösung.
   b) to feed – füttern
   c) Beiße nicht die Hand, die dich füttert.
   d) Be grateful for help, say thank you when people help you.

5. **Haste makes waste.**
   a) Individuelle Lösung.
   b) haste – Hetze, Eile, die Unvorsicht mitbringt; waste – Abfall, Verlust
   c) Eile mit Weile.
   d) Take the time you need to do things well. If you don't take your time, you will make mistakes.

6. **Too many cooks spoil the broth.**
   a) Individuelle Lösung.
   b) to spoil – verderben; broth – eine Art Eintopf, häufig mit mit Gemüse und Reis
   c) Zu viele Köche verderben den Brei.
   d) When too many people work on the same task, it is not effective. They will talk too much and won't find a quick and good answer.

7. **When life gives you lemons, make lemonade.**
   a) Individuelle Lösung.
   b) keine
   c) *aus dem Englischen/Amerikanischen inzwischen eingedeutscht:* Gibt dir das Leben Zitronen, mache Limonade daraus.
   d) You can do something with the things you've got. Don't be sad about the little/bad things you've got, use these things for a good cause.

8. **Every cloud has a silver lining.**
   a) Individuelle Lösung.
   b) lining – Rand, Begrenzung
   c) Auf Regen folgt Sonnenschein! In allem Schlechten liegt das Gute im Ansatz verborgen! Wo Schatten ist, ist auch Licht.
   d) After every dark and sad time, there will be a time of happiness. Don't worry about the sad things in your life, there will be better times waiting for you.

Unit 3

3.1 Focus on words: Sport

a) Crossword solution:
- 1 down: GOALKEEPER
- 2 across: PENALTY
- 3 down: EQUALIZE
- 4 down: TRAINING
- 5 across: COACH
- 6 down: HOUR (COURT)
- 7 across: CUP
- 8 down: SWIMSUIT
- 9 down: GOAL
- 10 across: FINAL
- 11 across: SUPPORTER
- 12 down: REFEREE
- 13 across: HELMET
- 14 across: SCORE

b) Teilweise individuelle Lösungen.

equipment	location	people	other
helmet, cup, swimsuit, goal, saddle, swimming trunks, badminton racket, skis, table tennis bat, …	court, ski slope, sports hall, running track, (swimming) pool, bridle path, half-pipe, pitch, …	goalkeeper, coach, to train, supporter, referee, equalize, tennis player, …	penalty, score, final, half-time, defence, training session, …

3.2 Focus on grammar: Relative clauses
a) An elephant is an animal **which** lives in Africa and Asia.
A teacher is someone **who** works in a school.
Chalk is something **which** writes white on a black board.
The internet is something **which** helps you to find important information.
A map **is something that helps you find your way.**
A referee **is someone who controls the players in a football match.**
A car **is something that takes you from one place to another.**
A shop assistant **is someone who sells something in a shop.**

b) Toby and Fiona are friends **who** have gone to school together for years. Now Toby's father, **who** works at a bank, has found a new job in Cardiff. So the Peterson family has to move. Toby, **who** likes his home town Canterbury very much, is sad. "Canterbury has got a great football team, all my friends live here – I even like my school! I don't even know what I will miss most", he says angrily. So Fiona has got an idea: she wants to have a farewell party. She invites the people **who** have been friends with the Petersons for years. Everybody **who** comes prepares something to eat **which** the Petersons like very much.
The evening of the party has arrived: The Petersons don't know anything about the party **which** is about to start any minute now. Fiona rings the bell and Mr Peterson, **who** looks very tired because of all the packing, opens the door. "Surprise" Fiona shouts, and all the friends **who** are invited, come round the corner. Mr Peterson calls his wife and children, **who** have been sitting in the empty living room. They can't believe it. They now know that they will miss their friends most!

3.3 Focus on grammar: Contact clauses
a) **Rule:** If who, which or that is the **object** of the relative clause, you can leave it out. You call these relative clauses **contact** clauses.
If who, which or that is followed by a **verb**, it is the **subject** and you cannot leave it out!

b)
1. Look at Sharon's earrings she made herself.
2. The train which is late arrives on platform 3.
3. There are many cars which drive too fast.
4. We went to a concert which took place in the concert hall.
5. London is a city Toby loves very much.
6. Tiger is a beautiful cat Ella's father bought for her.
7. We are too late which is not very nice of us.
8. I read an exciting book my mom bought for me.
9. You are a great friend I like very much.
10. Mowgli is a little boy who lives in the jungle.

3.4 Focus on grammar and writing: The passive voice
a) Football or soccer **is** a team sport that **is played** between two teams of eleven players. It **is seen** as the most popular sport in the world by many people. Football **is played** on a rectangular grass field with a goal at each of the short ends. The aim of the game **is** to kick a ball into the opposing goal.
Only the goalkeepers **are allowed** to touch the ball with their hands or arms, the rest of the team normally **kick** the ball with their feet. Although players usually **use** their feet to move the ball around, they may **touch** the ball with any part of their bodies other than their hands or arms. When the ball **is hit** by the player's head, it **is called** a header.
Physical contact between the players of the opposing teams **is forbidden**. The referee can **stop** the match when a player **is fouled** by another one and the match **continues/is continued** after a free kick or a yellow or red card for very hard fouls.
The team that **scores** the most goals by the end of the match **wins**. If both teams **have scored** an equal number of goals then the game **is** a draw. You **play** for 90 minutes and **have** a break of 15 minutes in between. After the break the teams **change** sides.

b) + c)
Individuelle Lösungen.

3.5 Test your knowledge
1	was born	m)
2	was sung	a)
3	was written	n)
4	was trained	c)
5	was won	h)
6	was built	e)
7	was invented	s)
8	was given	t)
9	was discovered	e)
10	was said	r)

Solution: Manchester

3.6 Writing a report on your last class trip
a) + b)
Individuelle Lösungen.

Unit 4

4.1 A crossword on Canada

Across/Down answers:
- WAY OF LIFE
- POPULATION
- VANCOUVER
- QUEBEC
- LACROSSE
- CANOE
- NATION
- FRENCH
- FISHERMAN
- LOCAL
- CAMPGROUND
- OTTAWA
- HURON
- SQUARE
- INUIT
- RANGER
- HOCKEY

4.2 Revision: The passive

a) Dragon boats **are** an old Chinese tradition. But they **can also be found** in Canada. They **are** very popular here. In Toronto, there **are** 20000 dragon boaters. Every year, a festival with many dragon boat races **is organized**. Dragon boats are canoes which **are decorated** with dragons' heads. They **are steered** by one person only, but there are 20 people in one boat who **paddle**. It is important that the crew **paddle** at the same speed. In the training session, many people **join** the crews. The training **goes on** for weeks and weeks. The race itself **is** only 200m long, but it is very hard.

Once the dragon boats **reach** the finish line, the dragon boaters **are celebrated** by the audience. They **clap** their hands and **shout** the teams' names. Each dragon boat team **has** their own fan club with posters and flags. The day of the race **is** something special for everybody – for those who are paddling as well as for those who are watching.

b) A bicycle was stolen. The pizza was taken out of the oven/was made. Ice hockey is played in Canada. Criminals are caught by the police. *Kingkong* is shown at the cinema tonight. Music is (often, normally) played at parties.

4.3 Focus on grammar: Simple past and past perfect

a) A few weeks ago I **went** to Canada on holiday with my family. We **had never been** there before, so everything was exciting and new. But the most exciting moment **was** when I first **met** Anna. She **stayed** at the same hotel. I **saw** her in the restaurant. Our eyes **met** but when I **wanted** to talk to her, somebody else **had been** faster than me. It was Scott, who **was staying** at the same hotel. This **was** the moment when our stupid competition **began**.

We **started** little games to impress Anna. First, we **climbed** up a mountain from different starting points. When I finally **got** to the top of it, Scott **had already** arrived. Proudly he **was taking** photos of himself at the cross. Next, we **went fishing**. When I **wanted** to show Anna the fish I **had caught**, Scott **had been** already at her side with a fish twice as big as mine in his hand.

Then I **had** a brilliant idea. I **went** to the local cinema to buy two tickets for the latest romance with Brad Pitt. When I **arrived** at the ticket office, of course, all the tickets **had been sold out**. Guess, who **had got** the last two tickets? You're right, it was Scott! The next morning I **bought** a nice bunch of flowers for Anna. I **knocked** at her door and when she **opened** it, somebody else **had already given** her a massive bunch of red roses. Yuck!

That **was** the moment when I **decided** to stop that ridiculous game. I **had** a nice day. I **went swimming**, **slept** in the sun and in the evening I **made** a fire, which I **had collected** some wood for in the afternoon. When I **was sitting** by the fire, suddenly somebody **sat down** next to me. It **was** Anna. She **took** my hand, **smiled** at me and we **had** a wonderful evening. We **spent** the rest of the time together. Scott **was quickly forgotten** …

b) Individuelle Lösungen.

4.4 Focus on grammar: Indirect speech

Jennifer wanted to know if Amber had seen Frank.
Amber said that she saw him. He was talking to me all the time.
Jennifer asked if I was one of his classmates from Barrington Grammar School.
Amber told her that I had been Miss Barrington the year before.
Jennifer said that I looked good. She asked if Amber thought I would ask Frank out on a date.
Amber said that she didn't think so because I had a boyfriend named Fred.
Jennifer told her that he was your boyfriend and that you were my best friend.
Amber said that she was going to ask Frank out at once.
Jennifer thought that this was a good idea but she wanted to eat some sausages first.

4.5 Mediation: A Telephone conversation

Individuelle Lösungen, hier ist eine mögliche:
1. It's nice hearing from you.
2. I am playing on my computer at the moment. What are you doing, Simon?
3. I love watching quiz shows. My favourite show is „Wer wird Millionär".
4. The sun is shining. Today, I made a trip to the harbor on my bike.

5 Hamburg is a city in the north of Germany. It has about 1,800,000 inhabitants.
6 Hamburg is close to the North Sea. You can go on a boat trip around the harbour.
7 You can see many musicals, but also rock concerts.
8 I like to listen to Coldplay too, but I like the Red Hot Chili Peppers, too.
9 It was nice talking to you. I hope you were able to understand me, because I am not used to talking English on the telephone.
10 I understood you perfectly well, too. Can I call you again before my next English test? Then we could repeat the indirect speech together.

4.6 Writing a story
a)
1 Brainstorm ideas.
2 Write down every idea.
3 Choose the best ideas.
4 Structure your ideas in a mind map or a chart (use the 5 'Ws' and 'How').
5 Write the story in three parts: a beginning, a middle and an end.
6 Revise the story (read it, check for mistakes and correct them).

b) + c)
Individuelle Lösungen.

Unit 5

5.1 Focus on words: Music, stars and instruments
a)

A	C	A	R	E	E	R	B	X	S
L	S	E	M	F	I	E	I	S	L
N	E	T	R	A	C	K	O	T	O
C	L	A	S	S	I	C	G	E	H
H	C	S	D	K	P	A	R	R	E
P	E	V	R	Q	O	L	A	E	O
P	O	P	U	L	P	R	P	O	V
O	L	D	M	I	S	W	H	O	S
S	S	I	S	K	T	R	Y	E	O
K	T	F	T	M	A	I	L	A	P
T	R	R	I	L	T	N	P	R	E
P	I	T	C	W	I	S	I	T	R
L	N	P	K	B	O	E	P	C	A
E	G	Z	S	N	N	U	E	M	T

b) career, biography, stereo, opera, track, classic drumsticks, pop, string, pop station, pipe

c) Individuelle Lösungen.

5.2 Talking about oneself – my own biography
Individuelle Lösungen.

5.3 Focus on grammar: Reflexive pronouns and verbs
a) himself, herself, itself, yourselves, themselves

b)
1 Steven taught **himself** how to play the guitar.
2 Mrs Miller bought a nice bunch of flowers for **herself**.
3 You don't have to wash cats. They wash **themselves**.
4 "Mum and dad are out. So we cooked **ourselves** a nice meal."
5 "Don't look into your neighbours test! Think for **yourself**!"
6 "Oh dear. Nobody is answering the phone. So I have to talk to **myself**."

c) worry, relax, move, meet, hide, calm down, open, sit down, turn, wonder, feel, imagine, prepare, remember

d) The Weirdo family

The Weirdos are a normal family, at least that is what they think about **themselves**. But, dear reader, decide for **yourself**. Emily and Jonathan Weirdo got married 13 years ago and decided to buy **themselves** a pink house with yellow stripes. They have lived in it until now. They have three children: Ken, 12, who has taught **himself** to walk on his hands and turn at the same time, Lisa, 10, who gets dressed in the morning with her eyes closed and little Chris, 6, who always moves in slow motion.
Every morning they meet for breakfast in the kitchen and sit down under the kitchen table. Then they get ready for school or work. At school, the teachers don't worry about the strange behaviour of the kids any more and accept them the way they are. As both parents work during the day, the kids have to cook for **themselves**. Luckily, they never argue and live a weird, but happy life.

5.4 Modal substitutes: Can, must and may

a) **Josh:** Lisa, remember, you **must** show your ticket soon, so take it out now.
Lisa: Right, Josh, but … oh no! I forgot to take out the orange juice I bought on the way. I **must** show my bag to the security guard now and I think you **may not** take glass bottles inside.
Josh: Oh – but that's no problem. Look, there is a bottle bank over there. Oh dear, I need to go to the toilet, I hope there are some inside.
Lisa: Yes, you **can** go to the toilets in the hall, no problem. Do you mind if we have a sandwich before the concert starts? I am hungry and I think there's a bar inside, where you **can** eat something.
Josh: Of course, Lisa. (*ringring*) Oops – my mobile, it's still on. I **must** switch it off, otherwise I **cannot/may not** take it inside with me.
Lisa: That's right, Josh, that's why I left my camera at home, people **may not** take photos of the band during concerts. And that's very sad, because I would love to have a photo of Gerry from "The Wolves" and me …
Josh: Dream on, Lisa!

b) Im Textaufbau individuelle Lösungen möglich, hier ein Lösungsvorschlag:
We weren't allowed to take any cameras or mobile phones inside, so Josh had to switch off his mobile. Lisa wasn't allowed to take her orange juice bottle inside, as it was a glass bottle. We had to show our tickets at the entry and also our bags. They were controlled by the security. Josh needed to go to the toilet, so he could use the ones in the hall. Lisa was hungry and could buy a sandwich at the bar. When we were in the hall, the concert couldn't start, because of technical problems. But when they finally started, they played all the songs and the fans could sing all the texts. Gerry saw Lisa and waved her, but she wasn't allowed to come up on stage. Josh had to go to the toilet again, so he missed his favourite song. Lisa couldn't buy a T-Shirt of "The Wolves", because it was too expensive. When a cracker exploded in the back of the hall, technicians had to switch on the light. All in all, "The Wolves" could show everybody how great they are.

5.5 Focus on grammar: Conditional III
a) 1+c, 2+a, 3+e, 4+b, 5+d

b) Individuelle Lösungen.

c) Hier sind unterschiedliche Lösungen möglich:
If she hadn't gone to Hollywood, she **wouldn't have had a look at the studios.**
If she hadn't met Steven Spielberg, **she wouldn't have been able to talk to him.**
If Spielberg hadn't offered her a part in her film, **she wouldn't have met Brad Pitt and Kate Winslet.**
If Sarah hadn't met Brad Pitt and Kate Winslet, **she wouldn't have gone to their homes.**
If the film hadn't been a great success, **she wouldn't have won an Oscar.**
If the alarm clock hadn't gone off, **she would have dreamt on.**
If she hadn't gone to the school that day, **she wouldn't have met Jeff.**
9) 10) 11) Individuelle Lösungen.

5.6 Writing about a star

a) **Reporter:** Hello, **how are you**?
Lady GaGa: Fine, thank you.
Reporter: Great. So let's start with the questions. **What is your real name?**
Lady GaGa: My real name is Stefani Joanne Angelina Germanotta.
Reporter: Oh, that sounds Italian. **Are you from Italy?**
Lady GaGa: No, I'm not from Italy. I'm from Yonkers, New York in the USA. But my parents are Italian Americans.
Reporter: How old are you? And when is your birthday?
Lady GaGa: I'm 23 and I was born on 23rd March 1986.
Reporter: What do you do? What is your job?
Lady GaGa: I'm a singer, but I also wrote songs for stars like Fergie, Pussycat Dolls, Britney Spears and others.
Reporter: What was your first album called?
Lady GaGa: My first album was called *The Fame*.
Reporter: What are your greatest hits?
Lady GaGa: My greatest hits are "Just Dance" and "Poker Face".
Reporter: Do you play an instrument?
Lady GaGa: Yes, I learned to play the piano at the age of four.
Reporter: When did you write your first song?
Lady GaGa: I was 13 when I wrote my first song.
Reporter: Who is your best friend?
Lady GaGa: One of my best friends is Lady Starlight.
Reporter: Thanks for the interview. If your fans want to find out more about you, **what can they do**?
Lady GaGa: They can go to my official website. It's www.ladyGaGa.com.

b) Individuelle Lösungen.